Think by Design

Think by Design

Celebrating Design Thinking and Experiential Learning

Stacy Neier Beran, PhD

BEP
BUSINESS EXPERT PRESS
Leader in applied, concise business books

Think by Design: Celebrating Design Thinking and Experiential Learning

Copyright © Business Expert Press, LLC, 2024

Cover design by Alley Neary

Interior design by Exeter Premedia Services Private Ltd., Chennai, India

First published in 2024 by
Business Expert Press, LLC
222 East 46th Street, New York, NY 10017
www.businessexpertpress.com

ISBN-13: 978-1-63742-7-088 (paperback)
ISBN-13: 978-1-63742-7-095 (e-book)

Business Expert Press Marketing Collection

First edition: 2024

10 9 8 7 6 5 4 3 2 1

*To PinPoint Collective, for your curiously empathic and
positively optimistic determination to bring design perspectives
to others earlier and in unexpected experiences.
Thank you for coloring the equity conversation with empathy.
Thank you for reflecting back how great strategy begins with great research.
Thank you for always mirroring the vulnerability of
life's oh no and ah ha moments.*

Description

Uncertainty has an upside. In *Think by Design (TBD)*, you'll practice a hands-on approach to combine design thinking and experiential learning in business education. Our world's biggest challenges put pressure on everyone. These challenges require us to blend how we act with how we think. Through combined action and reflection, we learn to use what's yet to be determined as a problem-solving advantage.

TBD's methods and tools humanize problem-solving. Through four chapters, you'll practice design thinking in an experiential learning challenge characterized by authentic uncertainty. The challenge includes eight design thinking experiences and four retrospectives. Each chapter features a playful posture, used to activate core values. Templates and checklists equip you to collaborate using digital whiteboards. To close, you'll write a manifesto to prepare you for future challenges.

TBD acts as a unique primer for design thinking fundamentals. This book is perfect for business educators and students in experiential, interdisciplinary collaborations. Business practitioners who want to incorporate digital whiteboards will also find the templates and checklists actionable.

Contents

Testimonials

"The only thing more impressive than Dr. Neier Beran's ability to codify Design Thinking and Experiential Learning is how whimsically she does it. As a product professional with nearly 20 years of experience in the finance industry, I cannot overemphasize how important this book is for understanding how we actually solve problems. Grab this book with your HANDS, absorb it with your HEAD, and love it with your (whole) HEART! BONUS: If our future problem solvers are in Dr. Neier Beran's classroom, we're going to be fine."—**Patrick Cannizzaro, SVP + Manager of Products, Northern Trust Corporation**

"Shifting from traditional textbooks and lectures to a hands-on learning approach is crucial for addressing the world's complex challenges. Think by Design *provides an optimistic and accessible guide for elevating leaders in any industry, blending practical insights and methodologies with genuine care and humility for our future.*"—**Pamela Conrad, Founder, Climate Positive Design & Design Critic, Harvard Graduate School of Design**

Preface

To Be . . . Drab?

No doubt, you know your favorite color. Whether you love the countdown to Pantone's Color of the Year or prefer neutrals, knowing your favorite color isn't a heavy ask. To respond, you don't skip a beat. Even if it takes a moment, a few favorite options surface.

Individual experiences with color vary. Our unique physiological makeups influence our nuanced perspectives of colors' tints and tones. Your outlook on your favorite color is personal.

When I am asked about my favorite color, I fire off, "all of them." I wanted to be a color forecaster. The psychology of color fascinated me. I wanted to impact the design of brands and products through color. Knowing which colors people preferred was not enough. I wanted to explore *how* and *why* color changed people's experiences. Whose problems might colors help to solve?

This book is not about color theory.

Instead, we will explore how your personal truths, beliefs, and decisions *color* your worldviews. To experience a more colorful worldview, we'll take action using uncertainty. Uncertainty, or a state of not knowing *yet*, is an asset to use in solving problems. When we know how to work with it, we will see uncertainty as desirable. Let's trust uncertainty like we do our favorite color, ready to create vivid pictures. In this context, that vivid picture is the solution to a complex problem.

I did not pursue a color-forecasting career. Instead, for over 15 years, I've taught Experiential Learning courses in business. Experiential Learning is often described as learning by doing. It designs a space for active, collaborative problem-solving. Students, clients, and community members who commit to Experiential Learning color my worldview. They, like me, see Experiential Learning as a way to solve our world's biggest challenges.

Not just any old challenges. It was not a problem to name your favorite color. It was a certain choice. Yet the problems we practice in Experiential Learning involve uncertainty. These problems are kaleidoscopic. As a kaleidoscope's mirrors reflect many colors, Experiential Learning reflects many problems. Kaleidoscopic problems blend complex, colorful contexts shaped by controversial ideas and issues. These problems impact consumers, community members, policy makers, and more.

Before our practice with *Think by Design* begins, I have a confession. There is one color I do not love: drab. Drab shows up as a light olive brown blended with yellow. Almost immediately, drab smacks us with its downside. A Google Images search for "drab" returns images of faded curtains and dull clothing. Drab's definitions are uninviting: lacking brightness or interest, dull, cheerless, and boring. *The Secret Lives of Color*, a popular book that explores the histories of 75 colors, even excludes drab from its "color cabinet" (Snyder 2017). If you happened to name drab as your favorite color, please forgive my aversion!

Why I dislike drab links to my background as a business educator. Each academic year, Graduation Day carbonates me with Christmas-morning-level excitement. Graduation is a coveted milestone moment for students and their families. It evokes relief, joy, and gratitude. Successes and experiences pave hopeful paths ahead. Weeks before the official commencement ceremony, cap and gown pick-up days stir anticipation. Students strut around campus carrying packages of pressed polyester. They seem to vibrate with excitement from the simple act of acquiring their regalia.

Business students' packages come with an unexplained accessory— drab-colored tassels (and, for graduate students, drab-colored hoods). Drab is the official color of business regalia. Time-honored rites of passage, like the cap toss or tassel turn, incorporate *drab*. Drab seems ill-fitted to symbolize our business graduates' grandest ambitions. During a moment of celebrated achievement, drab is certainly an unambitious choice.

I always ask soon-to-be graduates a colorful question. One that grips me with uncertainty after all these years. One that evades a clear-cut answer.

Not wanting to be a killjoy, I ask: *Why do you think drab symbolizes business education?*

Before going down a Reddit rabbit hole (because *[Serious] Why is the College of Business tassel color DRAB???* exists, I checked), I want to use my uncertainty about drab's symbolism as an opportunity. Drab's connection to business commencements seems trivial, but it holds a deeper meaning. How might drab *mirror* an opportunity for business education to transform students' experiences? How might we de-drab business education?

Business students opt for higher education during a time of ongoing societal unrest. *Disasters, disorder, disarray.* Headlines calling for social justice reforms leave no industry, sector, or market untouched. People advocate for justice in health care, education, urban planning, technology, pharmaceuticals, finance, housing, social services, law enforcement, and countless other sectors. We hear them, often loud but *unclear—uncertain—*about how to take action. Such heartbreaking movements and marches are anything but drab. Business is not immune to these constant, uncertain upheavals. In fact, business is prone to absorb much of the fallout.

Our World's Best Kaleidoscopes

Our global polycrisis ushers in new ways of thinking about business *as unusual.* The Information Era gradually legitimized an age of expertise (Bell 2023). We must remember that experts also feel uncertain when faced with complex problems. Through unprecedented and normalized access to digital platforms and devices, we watch business experts attempt to solve complex problems on a global scale. When even expert thinking falls short, we turn to critical ignoring as an in-demand skill (Kozyreva et al. 2022). We need practice choosing which online information to ignore or put to good use.

Colorful, *real* problems do not behave like laser-cut puzzles. They instead function as our world's best kaleidoscopes. Kaleidoscopes produce their complex, colorful patterns through a mirror system. The mirrors' angles cast *reflections.* Each reflection is a distinct yet *abstract* picture, open to interpretation. Kaleidoscopes symbolize how we might seek *color* in our problems. They give us a lens to mirror back the possibility of colorful solutions.

To Be De-Drabbed

Let's de-drab business education by reshaping students' relationships with uncertainty. Instead of shying away from complex problems, we can guide them to seek colorful problems.

To achieve this, business education should prioritize Experiential Learning (EL). EL involves hands-on practice with people-centered problematic scenarios (Fink 1999). The purpose of EL is twofold. First, EL aims to immerse students first-hand in contexts facing authentic problems. EL also prepares students for their transitions into future workplaces. Students in EL courses can't hide from their relationships with uncertainty. As they outgrow initial preferences for drab problems, they expand their worldviews. Through consistent EL interactions, students gradually favor taking action *with* unrelenting uncertainties. *Today's workplaces demand this type of learner.*

EL only occurs sporadically in business education. When it does occur, its implementation varies. So, what's needed to secure EL's position in business education? Where learning exists, thinking emerges. To frame EL, we need to explore Design Thinking (DT).

Trying to define DT is itself an attempt to learn with uncertainty. IDEO, a global innovation consultancy, says, "There's no one definition of design thinking" (Design Thinking Frequently Asked Questions... | IDEO n.d.). Faith (2019) describes DT as "basically the scientific method, with better branding."

Here's how I define design thinking:

A collection of hands-heart-head experiences that use uncertainty to determine needs-based solutions

Hands-heart-head means that DT takes on challenges that impact humanity. In this context, the order of hands-heart-head matters. *Think by Design* depends on taking hands-on action first despite uncertain conditions. Then, we connect our actions to the emotional and practical drivers of how we think. With consistent practice, we trust our hands will sync with our hearts and heads. We'll see more about this mindset on pages xl to xlii.

Throughout *TBD*, we seek *then* solve uncertain problems with to be determined outcomes. Our purpose—our why—is to be learners within complex systems of unprecedented uncertainty. Let's shift from the drab status quo to celebrate colorful uncertainty.

Welcome to *Think by Design*.

Acknowledgments

Think by Design could easily be titled *Teach by Design*. The title "teacher" largely defines my professional identity, and I'm grateful for the many teachers who constantly inspire me.

Faith Hurley, Stacy Callighan, Ashley Mendelsohn, and Charlei Hebron: thank you for teaching me just how many "group hugs" can happen in a week when we share our voices. Happy Thursday!

Patrick Green: thank you for teaching me that where there's curiosity, there's also hope and imagination. You were the earliest champion for an undergraduate design thinking course, and I'm forever grateful to you for opening my teaching journey to all things experiential learning.

Alley Neary: you taught me so much more than Illustrator! The design thinking course would not be on its upward trajectory without your willingness to take risks and then figure out what it all means. Thank you for being my Cannonball Co-pilot!

Ray Benton, Eve Geroulis, Mike Welch, Al Gini, Carol Scheidenhelm, Stan Stasch, Terri Pigott, and Abby Salat: even though our daily journeys don't intertwine, your styles of teaching journey with me every time I step into a classroom. Randy Voss, not all teachers need classrooms. Thank you for teaching me how innovation is a perpetual classroom.

Christine Miller and Lauren Alexander, Co-Founders of Commonspace Collective: thank you for always cheering me on. You were the first to know about this project. Inspired by your journeys as business owners, you taught me to keep going. (Thomas Davison, you too!)

Sean Connolly and Caitlin Botsios, Co-Founders of Helix Chicago: your commitment to Chicago's youth teaches all of us how to show up with hands-first action. I deeply admire you.

Allison English and Alison Riazi: you taught me to breathe. Christy Pemrick: you taught me how to stay distracted. I can track breakthrough moments in this book to the brilliant themes (and playlists!) you share during Saturday morning vinyasa. Julie Bellis, you made me so much

Stronger. Marquis Johnson, when I felt totally drained, you provided a fountain of a bike I didn't think I could ride.

Scott Isenberg and the BEP Team: thank you for teaching me that patience is at the heart of book production. I appreciate your flexibility and commitment to everyone's unique writing processes.

Mike and Mary Jane Beran: you taught me the true joy of international wanderlust. Thanks to you, I wrote some of my favorite sections in Italy, Scotland, Sweden, Denmark, and Norway.

Teach by Design also means Twin by Design: Leigh, my number one fraternal counterpart, all is well. I hope a second edition is in our future.

Finally, to my husband Matt, for his dogged determination and irreplaceable sense of dad joke humor. In all the iterations of the *TBD* acronym, all credit goes to you for my favorite one. That even the *TBD* Manifesto shows up in our pup, Twombly the (French)Bull Dog.

Introduction

To Be Determined . . .

How important is it to reschedule the meeting? TBD . . .
How expensive will gas prices get? TBD . . .
How does AI work? TBD . . .

The acronym *TBD* ordinarily stands for *to be determined*. Or maybe you prefer *to be decided*. Our conversational use of *TBD* suggests uncertain outcomes impact our everyday lives. By designating a shortcut to say we *do not yet know, TBD* accounts for our *temporary* knowledge gaps. It holds our uncertainties at bay. Its open-endedness signals that more information is forthcoming.

In this book, *TBD* broadly stands for *think by design*. *TBD* models how to enthusiastically seek, experience, and celebrate the uncertainty inherent in our world's colorful problems. To think by design is to use uncertainty as an asset. We get to invest that asset in higher-quality learning and thinking experiences. In turn, these experiences influence an alternative approach to solving problems—one that strives to restore or establish equitable, sustainable, and ethical business practices.

TBD also stands for truths, beliefs, and decisions (tbds). What we *believe* to be *true* guides how we *defend* our *decisions*.* Our perspectives, worldviews, and outlooks form from our tbds. Combined, tbds describe epistemology, or how we know what we know. The term epistemology may not make breaking news or become a TikTok sensation. But it is a ubiquitous part of our everyday lives. Epistemology underscores our learning and thinking. It guides how we construct our worldviews and outlooks. Through epistemology, humankind maintains its capacity to shape new knowledge into original solutions. This new knowledge forms during a period of time characterized by not knowing. When solutions are *to be determined.*

---

* For readability, decisions and defenses are used interchangeably in tbds.

Uncertainty Is an Asset

While we de-drab business education, we also need to destigmatize uncertainty. As business-minded people, we demand accurate superforecasting. We also watch ineffective judgment of world events (Schoemaker and Tetlock 2016) result in infodemics of misinformation. News alerts about human rights, environmental crises, and space travel fascinate us. Yet how certain—or uncertain—are we about these complex topics? Do we accept headlines at face value? Do we skim a preferred source for high-level understanding? Do we *seek* knowledge by combining a variety of worldviews before we *solve* problems? Or, is it a little bit of all three?

Think of uncertainty as a temporary gap in knowledge. Hear the difference between "I do not know" and "I do not know *yet*." The timing of yet—a future moment—might be short or longer term. We are more capable of co-existing with not yet knowing than we know. Even with the dissonance brought on by not always knowing, humanity thrives nonetheless. That's a colorful story worth celebrating.

Uncertainty in Authentic Problems

When was the last time you heard yourself saying "no problem"? What inspired you to give that response? My version of "no problem" sounds more like, "If that's our worst problem, we're doing okay." (Always an optimist, I describe Optimism in Chapter 4.) Our drab default is to casually talk about problems in a way that diminishes perceived risks. We prefer to dismiss looming symptoms of trouble. These casual occurrences, however, are not authentic problems.

To experience *TBD*, we must encounter authentic problems characterized by authentic uncertainty. EL and DT make those encounters possible. Both focus on taking action with problems that lack one "right" answer. The difference we run into is how each refers to problems.

In EL, we refer to authentic problems as ill-structured problems. King and Kitchener (1994) explain ill-structured problems as:

- ☐ Unexplainable with a high degree of completeness
- ☐ Unanswerable with a high degree of certainty
- ☐ A source of disagreement among experts

When we learn with ill-structured problems, we "learn to construct and defend reasonable solutions" (King and Kitchener 1994). EL prioritizes these high-value, high-impact outcomes. Every problem experienced in EL is a Challenge. A Challenge is a real-world scenario that needs a real-world solution. It centers on people who face a colorful problem and deserve colorful solutions. With no answer key to check in the back of a stump textbook, we depend on people's tbds to move a Challenge forward.

In DT, we refer to authentic problems as wicked problems. First described by Horst Rittel in 1967, wicked problems are "multidimensional problems which are extremely complex" (Wong 2022). Buchanan (1992) suggests that what is wicked is also *indeterminate*. Norman and Stappers (2016) expand the label into "wicked complex-socio-technical problems."

Wicked problems lack certainty. They are always unique yet interconnected with other wicked problems. The appeal of wicked problems stems from their lack of one right or wrong solution. They welcome many explanations from many perspectives. That also means you can count on wicked problems to be ongoing. Spoiler alert: no solution will be finite.

Clock or Cloud

Here's one more visual to lock in how EL and DT incorporate authentic problems. If you could only aim our kaleidoscope at a clock or a cloud, which would you pick?

Decades ahead of today's polycrisis, Popper (1966) predicted our modern relationship with problem-solving. He categorized problems as either *clocks* or *clouds*. Clock problems tick with predictability. They follow linear, well-structured paths. Cloud problems float in dynamic, unpredictable ways. They follow nonlinear, ill-structured paths. Clouds act as a wickedly colorful counter to drab clocks.

Some learning requires retrieval activities that focus on *known knowns* and *well-defined* issues. For example, you interact with clock problems when you take a multiple-choice exam. Well-structured scenarios, like those test questions, help us reason with the correctness of a solution. In some learning contexts, clock problems make sense. In others, clock problems force untimely delays in learning and thinking about problem-solving.

Learning *from* clock problems often precedes learning *with* cloud problems. But it doesn't have to be that way. Combining EL and DT challenges that sequence. By promoting *earlier* interactions with cloud problems, EL and DT achieve higher impact sooner (Kuh 2008). The desired impact can build over time *throughout our learning journeys.*

Instead of clock problems, let's spend our time gazing at cloud problems. The urgency of today's cloud problems reminds us that time is up on watching clock problems. Our ways of learning and thinking shift when we face real problems, just like clouds shift overhead. We lack certainty about what shapes and patterns the clouds will reveal. (Will you see the shape of your favorite emoji while I see my French Bulldog's face?) But we gain an alternate route to solve problems using our diverse tbds.

Authentic problems are universally experienced. Take The Global Goals. Described as "The World's To Do List" (Fealy 2022), 17 issues touch every global community. The list includes issues like gender equality, quality education, climate action, and responsible consumption and production. While the United Nations continually adjusts targets, "results have not matched the rhetoric" (Kristof 2023). The list remains undone. In other words, even The Global Goals' solutions are *to be determined.*

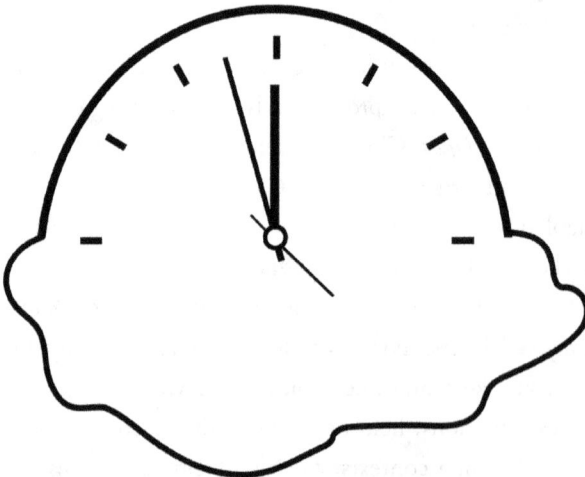

Figure I.1 Less clock watching and more cloud gazing

Authentic problems impact *all of us*. All of us can seek to impact authentic problems. Whether you label authentic problems as ill-structured, wicked, or cloud, problems in EL and DT are two sides of the same colorful coin. These problems are not drab. They are kaleidoscopic. The pages ahead use *colorful problems* to reflect the spirit of this concept.

All Diamonds Point to Reflective Thinking

Let's again return to our kaleidoscope. Imagine its most intricate, diamond-shaped configurations. Can you picture the diamonds dancing together? Their outward and inward movement choreographed by the turn of a dial? No matter what scale and colors reflect back, patterns of connected diamonds put on a show.

To de-drab the type of problem we see in business education, we need to de-drab our thinking style too. There's a colorful parallel between a kaleidoscope's reflections and our tbds. On page xv, we read that a system of mirrors makes possible the reflections we see in a kaleidoscope. These reflections mirror the "shade" of thinking we'll use throughout *TBD*. In business education, we default to critical thinking or analytical thinking to solve problems (Blijlevens 2021). In *TBD*, we practice reflective thinking to seek and solve problems.

Reflective thinking focuses on how our tbds evolve as we take action to seek then solve problems. Through reflective thinking, we accept our uncertainty about diverse, sometimes contradictory, worldviews. We use that acceptance to construct new ways of knowing and revise our tbds. Our revised tbds then rework our steps to problem-seek before we problem-solve.

We've all been there. We swoop in on a Challenge with good intentions yet misstep into misdiagnosis. This happens when we prefer to altogether bypass uncomfortable uncertainties.

Reflective thinking leads us to seek the problem before we solve the problem. Our natural tendencies to get swept away solving assumed problems dissipate. We become skilled at identifying actual colorful problems. As the world recalibrates around us, we must incorporate this type of thinking.

Here's the colorful twist about reflective thinking: it occurs when we take action in the context of colorful problems. We need regular practice with these problems to fast-track our reflective thinking. As we experience authentic uncertainty, our capabilities for reflective thinking evolve. Colorful problems ready us for reflective thinking.

To Be Doubled

We can use the perimeters of the diamonds viewed in a kaleidoscope to help us visualize how reflective thinking occurs. What's ahead multiplies the Design Council's Double Diamond method (Taylor 2021). For two decades, the Double Diamond has been a go-to framework to solve business problems. Two connected diamonds trace two thinking phases and four actions. Each diamond outlines both phases of thinking and two of the four actions. The left diamond's actions are *to discover* and *to define*. The right diamond's actions are *to develop* and *to deliver*. We'll experience each of these actions in the chapters ahead.

The Design Council transparently discusses the framework's limitations: "the ascendance of fast-paced digital design, along with the complexities of the challenges designers are currently addressing with services and systems, have left the Double Diamond a bit short of breath" (Eisermann, n.d.). Business practitioners eager to carry the Double Diamond's legacy forward propose reimagined versions. A Double Diamond 4.0. for, example, proposes how to integrate AI with the model's fundamental features (Yeo 2023).

TBD incorporates its own 4.0 interpretation but with *four* diamonds. To ensure problem-seeking precedes solving, *TBD* doubles the Double Diamond. Seeking actions distinguish Diamonds One and Two. Solving actions distinguish Diamonds Three and Four. All four diamonds point to reflective thinking, a dimension not included in the original model.

What makes reflective thinking colorful is its adaptability to other types of thinking. Red and blue mix to create purple. Yellow and blue mix to create green. In *TBD*, *divergent thinking and discerning thinking mix to create reflective thinking.*

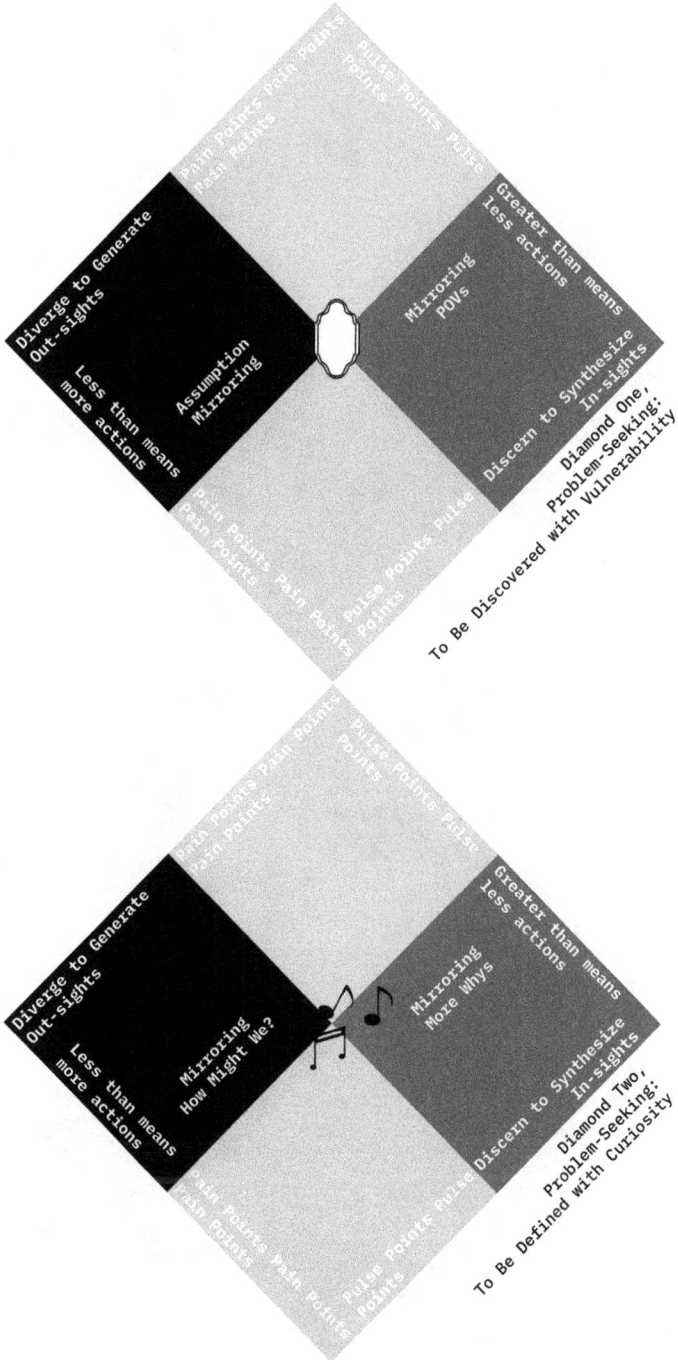

Figure I.2 To Be Doubled: The Double Double Diamond

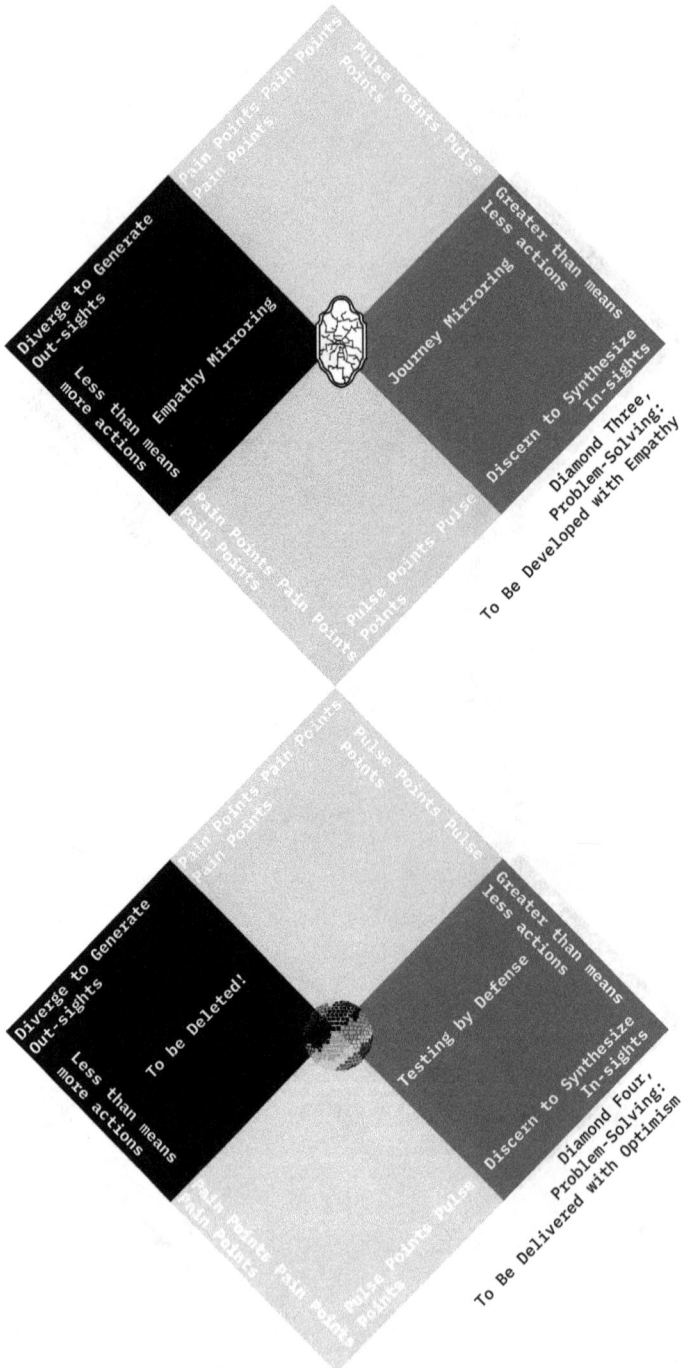

Figure I.2 (Continued)

Diverge Out-Sight: Less Than Means More

The left side of a diamond, shaped like a less than sign, outlines divergent thinking. Divergent thinking drives how you visualize your initial responses to a colorful problem. Divergent thinking often includes high levels of abstraction and abundant uncertainty.

Don't let the less than sign trick you. When you diverge, you generate. Divergent thinking happens when we generate *more* truths, beliefs, and defenses. Emphasize *generate*. Let your thinking go wide, as the outward-pointing less than sign directs. Generate ideas, questions, comments, remarks, images, references, and any other relevant concepts. *Less than means more.* Forget the drab "think outside the box" idiom. Instead, diverge to stretch your learning and thinking to the diamond's edge.

Diverging along that outward angle may feel overwhelming or intimidating. It can feel like there's no horizon line to limit how far you diverge. Where do you start? When do you stop? Taking action to learn and think in different ways comes with discomfort. Because we've learned to clock watch, we don't immediately trust the shift to cloud gaze.

Natural concerns like these materialize as pain points. Think of pain points as the difficulty or tension you experience as you move from drab ways of knowing into colorful ways of reflecting. Pain points push our willingness to act beyond the Challenge's immediate context. They stretch us to look for indirect connections and aspirational influences.

When you diverge with—not *against*—pain points, you visualize as many options as you can. Divergent thinking allows us to instinctively work with what we know to reveal what we don't yet know. You have permission to stretch your ways of knowing, even when that stretch brings impermanent pain points.

To ease this pain, keep your *sight* set *out*. When you fully diverge, you generate "out-sights." Out-sights are the outcome of the ongoing generative actions made possible by diverging outside. Out-sights show you the range of perspectives you can associate with the Challenge.

Think of a time when you let yourself get lost online. Did you search for one thing and find something unexpected that inspired you? Everything you noticed, observed, clicked, saved, and bookmarked on that scroll session was an out-sight. Out-sights document your "less than is more" actions, as random as they at first appear. Even the most disjointed finds can help us to move forward into the counterpart to diverge.

Discern In-Sight: Greater Than Means Less

The right side of the diamond, shaped like a greater than sign, outlines discerning thinking. Discerning thinking drives how you synthesize the out-sights generated by divergent thinking. Discerning thinking decreases uncertainty and transforms fewer, more relevant out-sights into usable perspectives.

Again, don't let the greater than sign trick you. When you discern, you synthesize. Discerning thinking happens when we reveal new perspectives from out-sights already generated. Emphasize *synthesize*. Discern follows diverge to combine out-sights into higher-quality tbds about future actions. Hone your thinking, like the inward-pointing greater than sign directs. Synthesize your reasoning by building from what you've already generated. You again push your thinking to the diamond's edge but downward to a sharper point. As you approach the greater-than edge, your tbds become less uncertain.

On the discern side of the diamond, we work with pulse points. Think of pulse points as gut or reality checks that follow pain points. When we discern a pulse point, we check on our progress to synthesize sharper perspectives. Pulse points push us to think deep inside the Challenge and uncover meaning among our out-sights.

To optimize pulse points, keep your *sight* set *in*. When you fully discern, you synthesize "in-sights." In-sights are the outcome of the ongoing evaluation made possible by discerning thinking. In-sights show *how* and *why* you make connections from *what* your out-sights revealed. Through in-sights, we transform scattered views into actionable outlooks that influence reflective thinking.

Outward pain points lead to inward pulse points. This sequence shapes each of the chapters ahead into a diamond. Four chapters means four diamonds link together. But what secures that link? Diverge and discern happen *within* the four diamonds' edges. What happens where two diamonds' edges touch? What happens when Chapter 1's discern side connects to Chapter 2's diverge side?

Pause at the Pinch Point.   With all this thinking about divergent and discerning thinking, where is reflective thinking?

Reflective thinking stares back at us when we reframe an easily overlooked detail. When Chapter 1's discern side continues on to Chapter 2's diverge side, reflective thinking happens. Reflective thinking occurs at the pinch point between the diamonds, where you validate how your tbds have changed. Think of a pinch point like a growing pain. You've grown from being full of thought to being more thoughtful. Just when you've synthesized the pulse points, the pinch point alerts you to new pain points ahead.

Pause to reflect at pinch points. Validate how your tbds are changing. As you'll see, each chapter's format makes that pause a reality.

Framing Each Chapter

To make thinking about thinking less abstract, let's look at the actions you'll experience. The four chapters ahead will prompt you to take immediate action. Use the chapters as your playbook to practice *Think by Design*.

To Be Deconstructed: Reframing Your Reading Experience

Act Then Reflect.   The format of *Think by Design* reframes your reading experience.

Think about the layout and content of a traditional textbook. Its format supports well-structured problems and downplays learning by doing.

The format of *TBD* takes advantage of that opportunity. Each chapter will immediately inspire your actions *while you experience not knowing yet*. To reframe the reading experience, expect sections that deconstruct traditional presentation of content.

Too often, we undercut our readiness to act by overthinking. We back our way into action only after excessive time on the sidelines. Traditional book formats prolong our time on those sidelines. We spend abundant time studying explanations of theoretical problems. We scan case study sidebars, often stories presented as fictional vignettes. In our world of high-alert headlines though, traditional clock problems lack real-time relevancy. We spend our already limited time on negotiating what to do instead of the actual doing.

TBD wastes no time in putting our hands to action. EL exemplifies regular, hands-on encounters with colorful problems. DT also takes advantage of continuous actions within limited time frames. Design sprints, or outcome-oriented ways "to make really great progress on a challenge in a relatively short amount of time" (How to Use Sprints to Work Smart and Upskill, 2022), frequently shape how teams go full speed ahead to solve problems.

Each chapter includes three sections, Diverge, Discern, and Reflect. Within these sections, actions *precede* reflections. Actions, called Experiences, represent our *how*. Reflections, called Retrospectives, represent our *why*. Actions are to Experiences as reflections are to Retrospectives. This sequence means we carry forward what we already experienced into how we look back in retrospect. This is more than retracing steps to achieve "hindsight is 20/20" convenience. Retrospectives re-expose you to the uncertainty you've experienced.

Within each section, subheadings repeat across chapters. Duplicated subheadings are a deliberate, iterative way to see *TBD* as a process to practice. To iterate is to repeat a process using the output of your first practice to start your next practice. As you iterate, your commitment to *act then reflect* strengthens. You drill deeper into how and why you can defend what you believe to be true. Deconstruct the drab idiom "practice makes perfect" into "iteration takes imperfect practice."

To Be Delimited. Action-oriented checklists in each major section ease you into this imperfect practice. These checklists organize the deconstructed reading experience. They also delimit: they list specific constraints that shape your actions and reflections. Constraints describe the conditions needed for fewer but better actions and reflections. When we work with (not against) checklist constraints, we more deeply explore our tbds. Constraints make the space we need to see our tbds evolve as we iterate in real time. Constraints do not *limit* us. They do not enforce boundaries but establish "creativity guardrails" (Constraints in Design, n.d.).

Postures. It's easy enough to say that we'll keep a hands-first reframe top-of-mind. It's another thing to act on those positive intentions.

To keep you energized, each chapter features a recommended posture. Think of a posture as an attitude, lens, or stance you carry into each diamond. These postures operate as *TBD*'s values. Societal and business cultures both depend on values as guiding principles. Similarly, postures guide us to see a bigger purpose in our tbds. Postures situate you as you take what you learned from one diamond into the next. They also provide common ground for teams to unify their diverse perspectives.

Any time deconstruction stirs up doubts, depend on the chapter's posture to hold you steady.

Experiences: What to Expect.   The Diverge and Discern sections begin with an Experience. An Experience invites your team to take action through a series of steps that align with DT and EL. Sections labeled *Diverge to Generate* or *Discern to Synthesize* prompt how you interact with the Experience through a checklist of actions. Use these checklists as guidelines while you customize your actions. Take action using the order listed, yet also stay open to alternative orders. Maybe you want to combine steps into concurrent actions. Maybe you want to partially complete a few steps and then loop back around to finish what you started. Go top-down or bottom-up. There is no wrong way to take action during an Experience. No wrong way should sound familiar too. Colorful problems do not have wrong solutions or answers. Not worrying about what's wrong means we free our postures to take action at the diamonds' edges.

A To Be Discussed section follows each Experience. Overall, the goal of To Be Discussed is to practice *playbacks*. IBM defines playback as a time to "tell stories and exchange feedback about the work." Each discussion is a playback of the actions you just took. We play back the pain points involved with generating out-sights. We play back the pulse points involved with synthesizing in-sights. These discussions double-check our actions and ready us to transition into reflection.

A To Be Discussed checklist presents you with playback prompts to help you work with tbds not top-of-mind. What you discuss iterates something from the preceding Experience. Some playbacks guide you to add onto your Experience. Others prepare you for the next Experience or reflection.

Mirror Metaphors. As postures guide each Experience, metaphors illustrate each Retrospective. Metaphors, like postures, provide peace of mind while uncertainty remains top-of-mind. Metaphors link unrelated images to our iterations. These images also guide us to verbalize nonobvious tbds.

Metaphors, like mirrors, convey lightness and a sense of playfulness. The complexities of EL and DT Challenges can get weighty. A comparison to something unexpected yet familiar and concrete refocuses and reassures you. You can look to Mirror Metaphors to see familiarity coexist with uncertainty. Let Mirror Metaphors cut through confusion and reflect what drives your decision-making.

Retrospectives: What to Expect. A Retrospective (Retro) section follows the Experience sections. This section reflects back on the pain points and pulse points of the preceding Experiences. First, the Retro recaps the purpose, importance, or highlights of the Experiences. Describing the differentiating qualities of each Experience defogs uncertainty about actions already completed. Retrospectives then seek to validate how the Experiences moved the Challenge forward. Constraints guide you to see how your actions dovetail with evolving tbds.

Defogging your actions after you've experienced their outcomes seems counterintuitive. Yet this intentional order of operations benchmarks your reflective thinking. Through it, we compare our actual actions to what we now know about the theoretical ideal. You compare what happened to what you thought would happen. From that comparison, you make decisions about future actions using expanded truths and beliefs. Knowledge gained in retrospect de-drabs our usual pattern and defogs our next steps.

Finally, to end each chapter, Retrospectives backcast, or end with the start in mind. Backcasting invites you to "work backward from an imagined future state" (Krippendorff 2022). But how does that work, when you've been uncertain from the start? We'll pause and commit to immediately putting reflective thinking into action. When one chapter's pinch point dulls, the next chapter's pain points await.

A Framework That Works the Frame

Frames in Action.   To put the *TBD* framework to work, let's reframe what other contexts refer to as an artifact or deliverable. You create a Frame when you document your Experiences and Retrospectives. A Frame is a container to hold the output you produce based on checklist constraints. Drawings, sketches, images, text, outlines, and other relevant shapes count as output.

Frames do more than collect output. They form mirrors for you to visualize the blurry line between your actions and thinking. Each Frame reveals how your actions encounter uncertainty throughout each chapter.

In our photo-obsessed culture, we know a thing or two about framing our comings and goings. Here, those comings and goings are our acting and reflecting. Like you frame posts for favorite social media platforms, post your *TBD* Frames. Prepare Frames that are shareable for career portfolios, personal websites, and resumes. Frames demonstrate to workplaces how you contribute to collaborative efforts to solve problems. Frames also tell the whole story of your EL and DT practice. From pain to pulse to pinch points, Frames map the whole workflow of your EL and DT practice. That's a story worth sharing.

Reframe Mapping to Mirroring.   Speaking of maps, Frames deconstruct another concept common to DT. Popular DT frameworks integrate maps. Carter (2022) describes map as "a bucket term for information that's sorted spatially and depicted (even slightly) visually." Maps help us make sense of unfamiliar contexts, systems, experiences, and relationships. Through 2D visuals structured by relevant criteria, maps guide us to prioritize our thinking (Gibbons 2018). We can see what is missing from or entrenched in how we see relationships in entire systems.

To lean into this reframe, *TBD* swaps *maps* for *mirrors*. Mirrors, like colors, come in a variety of visual surfaces. Some mirrors appear like sparkling pools of water, so clear they display the full picture. Other mirrors have oxidized finishes. Their spotted contrasts reflect disjointed, partial pictures. This finish adds visual interest at the cost of an uninterrupted view. Both finishes produce their intended outcome: to reflect.

Yet reflections from these finishes are always susceptible to fog up. When the heat of our pain points collides with the cooling effect of our pulse points, things get foggy.

What happens when the mirror gets too foggy and obstructs a certain view of the whole picture? What happens when we can only see uncertainty reflect back?

To improve reflective thinking, we first need foggy reflections. These reflections depict our uncertainty. We aren't sure what lives past the foggy reflection, yet we trust the foggy reflection is temporary. One Experience and Retrospective at a time, we wipe away more fog from the Frame. We find a clearer—more certain—mirror reflection.

Colorful Whiteboards. A mirror shows you the actions you took but is not itself the tool. How might we document the entire *TBD* journey as Frames worth sharing? Let's reframe decision-making in boardrooms to collaborating on whiteboards. By using digital whiteboards, we access an in-demand tool to create colorful Frames.

Digital whiteboards support how we collaborate during each Experience and Retrospective. Online Software as a Service (SaaS) collaboration platforms like Miro, Mural and Figjam existed years before face-to-face workplaces transformed into flexible workspaces. Microsoft, Apple, Canva, and Zoom also integrate advanced whiteboard capabilities alongside their core functions. These technologies provide shared space to make learning and thinking visual. Visual communication is now an essential part of many jobs (Melendez 2023). Roles ranging from managers and engineers to researchers now include responsibilities that revolve around sharing visual ideas.

With workplaces in perpetual flux, whiteboard tools take on new significance. The transition from boardroom to whiteboard requires facilitation skills. These in-demand skills engage collaborations, interactions, and dialogue. This marks a shift from drab managing and presenting.

Facilitate Co-Design. When you use whiteboards to facilitate, you practice co-design. Co-design is how we relate to who we work with as equals. We frame fewer *selfies* and reflect more *ussies*. Through co-design, we distribute authority among our collaborators. This means we unlearn the power dynamics fixed in our follow-the-leader habits. We accept that no one is the expert. You teach others about your thinking and learning. Reciprocally, they teach you about their thinking and learning. We recognize and celebrate a range of perspectives, both spoken and unspoken. When you facilitate co-design, you inspire others to frame their outlooks through others' worldviews. We all assume the role of co-designer. We *teach by design* and practice *together by design*.

Think of whiteboards as space for co-design practice. Whiteboards allow us to visualize, iterate, critique, and experiment by incorporating all co-designers' outlooks. Everyone projects or screen-shares their tbds. Clusters of text, arrows, sketches, and other concrete output all are fair game for screen sharing. By visualizing everyone's uncertainty, you identify patterns of out-sights and in-sights. Anyone on #TeamDrab may read whiteboards as uncomfortably messy. #TeamColor, however, will co-design their whiteboards to reflect the whole, colorful story of our Challenge.

Whiteboards 101. Irrespective of SaaS brand, digital whiteboards include fundamental features that help you create Frames. Features used throughout Experiences and Retrospectives include:

- ☐ **Workspace**: The wide-open, limitless space where you document each chapter's Frames.
  - ☐ A workspace is the equivalent of a file.
  - ☐ A workspace holds everything you create and iterate during one whole Challenge.
  - ☐ Workspaces offer infinite room for collaboration and easy retrieval of work-in-progress Frames.
  - ☐ Like an art gallery, hang all your output on the virtual walls of your workspace.
- ☐ **Frame**: A container that holds or mirrors back each chapter's output.
  - ☐ A Frame is the equivalent of a page or worksheet in other tools.
  - ☐ Within one Frame, you'll mirror two Experiences and one Retrospective.
  - ☐ Aim for one Frame per chapter. You can add or combine Frames as you need to stay organized.

- □ **Mirror templates:** A customizable space to reflect back how you co-design with constraints.
  - □ Within the Frame, a mirror reflects back how you personalize your interaction with each Experience and Retrospective.
  - □ Each chapter includes templates for you to recreate and design mirrors that reflect your tbds.
- □ **Sticky notes:** Small pieces of digital paper used to visualize or document thinking; the building blocks of each Frame used to add dimension to mirrors.
  - □ Sticky notes appear throughout every Experience and Retrospective. Use sticky notes to externally express your thinking in action. Sticky note by sticky note, we reflect our actions to ourselves and others.
    - □ Look for sticky notes with:
      - □ Duplications, similarities, or overlaps: Does more than one sticky note communicate equivalent tbds?
      - □ Contradictions, contrast, or variation: Does more than one sticky note communicate incompatible tbds?
      - □ Mismatched ideas: Did some sticky notes end up with irrelevant constraints? Do sticky notes need to be shuffled?
  - □ All co-designers should aim for two to three sticky notes per constraint. This quantity is an estimate, not a hard rule.
  - □ Give co-designers a few quiet minutes to decide what to write on their sticky notes.
  - □ Anonymous sticky notes help to separate co-designers' identities from stigma surrounding controversial thoughts.
  - □ Move sticky notes within the Frame to locations relevant to checklist constraints. Drag and drop to relocate at any point.
  - □ Click to write text or use the workspace toolbar to sketch, connect, reshape, or add images and emojis.
  - □ Adjust sticky note colors as preferred. Colors can help you organize what goes into each Frame. You might use different colors per co-designer, for example. Some checklists incorporate the spirit of color psychology. You

might match the color of sticky notes to the color of the constraint.

☐ Make sticky notes simple, clear, articulated, easy to read, and summarized. Don't be afraid to use lots of sticky notes to avoid cramming too much thinking into one note.

☐ Use the whiteboard's duplicate or copy function to replicate original sticky notes as needed. Some checklists encourage you to apply existing notes to additional constraints. Keep the original notes to see your progress.

☐ Add sticky notes as often as you prefer, even if you aren't directly prompted by a checklist to do so.

As you facilitate whiteboard co-design, you'll find favorite features and shortcuts. Use what's instinctual. Without a singular clickstream to follow, the whiteboard is yours to design. You can explore training videos, micro-credential academies, and interactive communities for in-depth exploration. Nonetheless, here are a few pro facilitation tips:

☐ Whiteboards offer flexible options to integrate external images. Upload images from your device or explore photo search services for copyright-free photos. Sources like Unsplash and Pexels can be integrated into whiteboard tool bars.

☐ Whiteboards integrate timers. Each chapter ends with a three-minute activity. Set the timer within your workspace.

☐ Whiteboards feature dot voting, sometimes called sticker voting or dotmocracy. Dot voting lets you quickly tally what resonates among co-designers. It quantifies everyone's tbds at that moment. Some Experiences and Retrospectives guide you to select which out-sights and in-sights to carry into subsequent Frames. By dot voting, you eliminate what doesn't track with checklist constraints. In *TBD*, think of dot voting as drab voting.

☐ Cast your no vote with a drab dot. You see too many pain points to risk moving forward. Or, a constraint seems slightly off, leading you to see that a pulse point isn't sharp enough. Drop what earns drab dot votes from future decision-making.

- [] Drab dots, by process of elimination, also show your approval. You visualize and quantify everyone's preferences by what doesn't get a drab dot.
- [] Give one drab dot vote to each co-designer per constraint. Depending on how many co-designers share the whiteboard, expect Frames to become quite full, even messy, with lots of drab dots. Take that as a sign that something much more colorful is underway.
    - [] To consolidate, vote together as co-designers. Continue to be thoughtful about group think by again allocating a few quiet minutes for co-designers to first choose their vote.
- [] As preferred, highlight what doesn't receive drab dots. Use emojis, colorful dots, or other whiteboard tools to mark what moves ahead.

Whole Human Mindset

That's it, the whole *Think by Design* roadmap. Well, almost.

One last detail makes all of this whole. You.

I invite you, as a whole human, to Think by Design. Allow your whole person to practice how to experience uncertainty. EL and DT focus on the humans involved in a Challenge's complexities. *You are one of these humans.* For any of this to be meaningful, you—the *whole* you—must show up. *Diverge to be full of thought. Discern to be thoughtful.* Trust your actions as reflections of how and why you think with uncertainty, not what you overthink for accuracy.

If it seems like my head is in the clouds, daydreaming through a kaleidoscope, good! That's me, how I show up as a whole human. Double-click into this wholesome woo, and you'll see I sync my hands and heart with my head-in-the-clouds approach. This is the *whole human mindset* at practice.

Your hands for action, heart for the world, and head for business form the Whole Human Mindset. In retrospect, *TBD*'s definition of design thinking (on page xvi) also dropped a significant clue.

I also think of the Whole Human Mindset as the space where our professional and personal identities break even. As business-oriented people, we may not run into deliberate opportunities to practice mindsets. Yet, businesses increasingly acknowledge mindset as a unifying element of company culture. IDEO calls out mindset as "the intention we carry with us into our projects" (Stafford and Suri 2021). SAP, a global enterprise SaaS firm, sees mindset as "a way of being" (Maghraby and Oswald 2021). Salesforce, the world's leading CRM organization, views mindset as "a collection of beliefs that guide and shape our habits" (Miller 2020). Organizations like these depend on their employees to show up as whole humans.

To inspire your Whole Human Mindset, let's dispel common mindset myths.

There is more to mindset than its pop culture reputation suggests. Whether perceived as a wellness fad or an 80s poster-turned-throwback-meme, mindset matters. In confronting the "hang in there" motto seen on stuck kitten posters (you know the one), Victore (2019) offers a call to action made for mindsets. "Let go, kitty!" The uncertain action of "let go" unclenches our *hands*. It also relaxes our *hearts* and *heads*—our whole human—to more deeply reflect. *Act, then reflect.* Mindsets give us permission to let go of controlled, drab certainty. A mindset, then, is like perpetual insurance coverage to protect your "let go" landing. (I bet the kitten on the original poster had pet insurance!)

In *TBD*, a mindset behaves like that insurance policy. It protects our learning and thinking amidst uncertainty throughout the process. When we let go of entrenched certainties, we depend on our tbds to stick the landing at every pain, pulse, and pinch point along the way.

The Whole Human Mindset combines how we act (hands), feel (heart), and think (head). Singleton (2015) suggests that symbolizing human heads, hearts, and hands support transformative, values-based behavioral changes. Sipos, Battisti, and Grimm (2008) also confirm our natural capabilities to use our head to engage, our heart to enable, and our hands to enact. Hambeukers (2020) describes "all three levels working in unity" as what good design is all about. The American Institute of Graphic Arts (AIGA) believes in balancing head, heart, and hand to practice strategy, empathy, and craft, respectively (Grefe 2012).

How *TBD* differentiates from existing uses of head, heart, hands comes down to a subtle reframe. Hands always come first, moving heads to third place. Act, then reflect. Hands-first actions normalize how we digest the uneasy tensions in EL and DT. With practice, the doing of our hands reaches our feeling hearts and thinking heads, convincing us to use uncertainty as an asset.

From TBD to TL;DR (Too Long; Didn't Read)

Wow, that introduced a whole lot. Lucky for us, *TBD* looks a whole lot like *TL;DR. In retrospect,* scan this outline to validate the Introduction, kick-starting your *TBD* practice.

- ☐ Chapter 1: To Be Discovered With Vulnerability
  - ☐ In Chapter 1, we frame how to discover the problem by taking a posture of vulnerability. We will mirror:
    - ☐ Experience One: Diverge to discover your pre-Challenge assumptions.
    - ☐ Experience Two: Discern to discover your Challenge Points of View (POVs).
    - ☐ Retrospective: Reflect through Beginner's Mirror to discover how to reframe collecting data.
- ☐ Chapter 2: To Be Defined With Curiosity
  - ☐ In Chapter 2, we frame how to define the problem through a posture of curiosity. We will mirror:
    - ☐ Experience One: Diverge to define options for what the problem might be.
    - ☐ Experience Two: Discern to define why the problem exists.
    - ☐ Retrospective: Reflect through Musical Mirror to define one priority problem.
- ☐ Chapter 3: To Be Developed With Empathy
  - ☐ In Chapter 3, we frame how to develop solutions through a posture of empathy. We will mirror:
    - ☐ Experience One: Diverge to develop understanding about who the problem impacts.
    - ☐ Experience Two: Discern to develop how the problem integrates into everyday journeys.

☐ Retrospective: Reflect through Broken Mirror to develop unexplored solutions.
☐ Chapter 4: To Be Delivered With Optimism
  ☐ In Chapter 4, we frame how to deliver solutions through a posture of optimism. We will mirror:
    ☐ Experience One: Diverge to deliver a concrete consideration set of colorful solutions.
    ☐ Experience Two: Discern to deliver understanding about the impact of each solution.
    ☐ Retrospective: Reflect through Disco Ball Mirror to deliver low-fidelity prototypes of recommended solutions.

In the Closing Retrospective, we frame how to determine Mirror Manifestos.

☐ We will mirror:
  ☐ MAYA (Most Advanced Yet Acceptable) principles
  ☐ Metacognition, reflecting on our thinking
  ☐ Celebrations of *TBD*-inspired Manifestos

CHAPTER 1

To Be Discovered
With Vulnerability

Think of a Challenge that made your heart rate escalate. Do clammy hands and foggy headspace sound familiar? If you could hold up a mirror to yourself in that scenario, what would reflect back? If you were to draw that moment on a whiteboard, what would it look like? What surrounded you? What were you doing? How did those physical reactions to feeling vulnerable change your actions? Did vulnerability come to mind?

With vulnerability as our posture, Chapter 1 introduces us to the Discover Diamond. This is the first of our two problem-seeking diamonds. This phase of the Challenge puts us face-to-face with peak uncertainty. We need to *discover* a lot. Our current truths, beliefs, and decisions are all subject to be deconstructed and reframed. This state of not knowing yet may not be particularly comfortable, but let's *assume* it will be colorful.

To Be Discovered With Vulnerability

Vulnerability sounds unappealing. But it does not sound drab.

Many of us associate vulnerability with exposure to harm, danger, or hazard. We see vulnerability as an undesirable state of uncertainty with unlimited risks.

Society continues to evolve its views on vulnerability. Vulnerability equips us with more than hypervigilance to guard against threats and warnings. We are challenging traditional, often limiting, views that associate vulnerability with weakness. We are instead reframing vulnerability as a strength to use to our advantage. Through a posture of vulnerability, we can discover the inextricable link to uncertainty. That relationship provides vital input for problem-seeking.

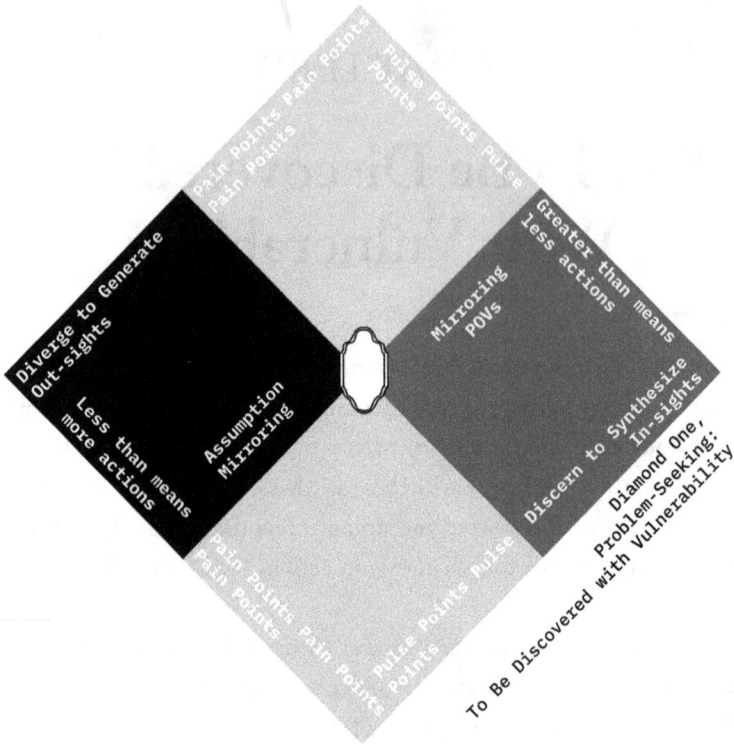

Figure 1.1 Diamond One: To be discovered with vulnerability

What Vulnerability Means in Think by Design

Vulnerability is a posture of openness. Starting with vulnerability eases us into uncertainty. It elongates the runway to reflective thinking. In Chapter 1, vulnerability opens us to discover assumptions through our actions. That discovery means we reveal new outlooks that improve how we seek problems.

We fill our everyday lives with assumptions. When we make assumptions, we make attempts to project what happens in uncertain circumstances. Every time we use imperfect knowledge to explain our reasoning, we lead with assumptions. Given the widespread appreciation of clock problems, acknowledging our assumptions is vulnerability in action.

Accepting vulnerability as a strength takes practice. By practicing vulnerability, we familiarize ourselves with its benefits. Vulnerability shores up authentic trust in collaborators. Vulnerability gets us to embrace uncertainty as a permanent part of co-design. Through vulnerability, we become more susceptible to discovering new ways of knowing. Our willingness to learn improves.

All these benefits apply to our Challenge. Practicing vulnerability on its own can't remove uncertainty. But it can make us more disciplined in how we use our vulnerability to uncertainty as an advantage.

Add a Chapter 1 Frame to your whiteboard's workspace. Within this Frame, let's use Figures 1.2 and 1.3 as templates to practice together.

Experience: Assumption Mirroring

Hold up a mirror to any Challenge in business, and you'll observe many moving parts in context. We notice a mix of people and relationships; models and systems; infrastructures and transactions. Taking in the whole reflection of the current context matters. From it, we gain situational awareness of the broader operating environment. Such *context* offers an initial glimpse into organizational mission and values. It also helps to locate risky scenarios where uncertainty co-exists with colorful problems.

Now, imagine the mirror you hold up is foggy.

Even though we look at the Client's context, what do we actually see? We can't expect to discover a clear, certain reflection from a fogged-up mirror. Our foggy context mirrors layers of complexities, unknowns, and ambiguity. In that fog, the source of our colorful problem reflects back at us, ready to be discovered.

To make up for what we do not yet see but need to know, we make assumptions. Below the foggy mirror surface, we will discover how assumptions and uncertainty go hand-in-hand.

Diverge to Generate

Use Figure 1.2 to mirror your out-sights using less than means more actions.

1. Begin with a 2 × 2 grid.
   □ Label the X-axis *Knowledge.*

☐ Label the X-axis endpoints as Uncertain (left endpoint) to Certain (right endpoint).

☐ Label the Y-axis *Reasoning.*

☐ Label the Y-axis endpoints as Desirable (top endpoint) to Undesirable (bottom endpoint).

2. Use each quadrant to discover:

☐ Assumptions we bring *to* the Challenge, and

☐ Truths, beliefs, and decisions we lack and need to discover *during* the Challenge.

3. Start with the top right quadrant, To Be Drab (Certain + Desirable).

☐ All out-sights generated in each intersection must reflect *both* constraints listed.

☐ Some constraints might generate very similar assumptions. What's certain in the top right might also be certain in the top left. Push to discover what's unique when the second constraint comes into play.

4. Work clockwise from the top right to generate sticky notes in each intersection.

☐ Diverge out-sight To Be Drab (Certain + Desirable):

☐ Describe what we already know about our Challenge's context.

☐ Describe what instantly reflects back as true.

☐ Talk about current conditions or circumstances with positive outcomes.

☐ Brag about what you believe holds potential for positive impact.

☐ Diverge out-sight To Be Deferred (Certain + Undesirable):

☐ Describe what we already know about our Challenge's context.

☐ Describe what instantly reflects back as true.

☐ Talk about current conditions or circumstances with negative outcomes.

☐ Describe what instantly comes to mind about negative impacts we know to be true.

☐ Describe what you believe holds potential for negative impact.

☐ Diverge out-sight To Be Detrimental (Uncertain + Undesirable):

    ☐ Describe what we need to know about our Challenge's context.

    ☐ Brag about what we believe to be true.

    ☐ Talk about future decisions that could reflect negative impact.

☐ Diverge out-sight To Be Discovered (Uncertain + Desirable):

    ☐ Talk about what we don't know about our Challenge's context.

    ☐ Describe what truths we lack but want to know more about.

    ☐ Brag about what instantly reflects back as an opportunity for positive impact.

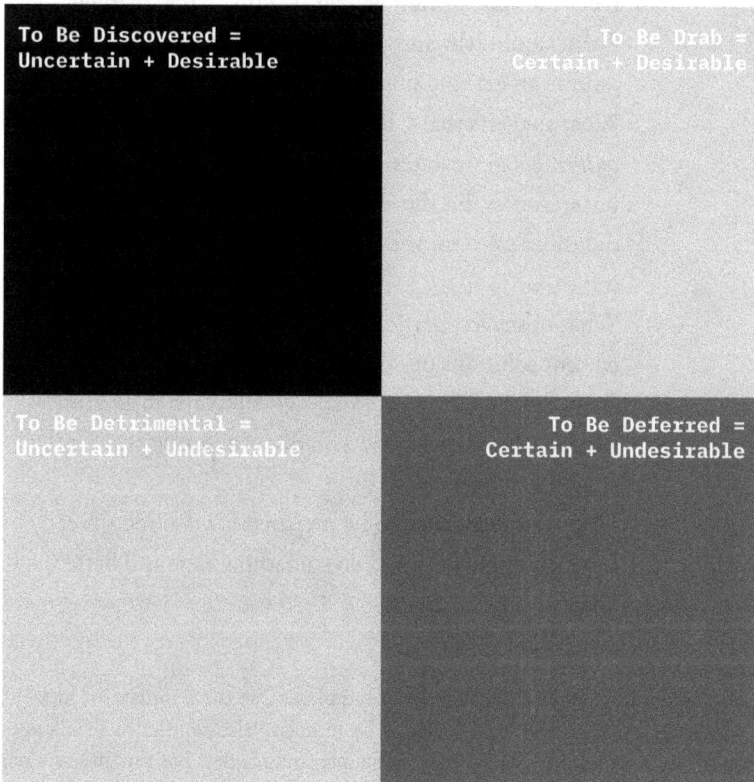

To Be Discovered = Uncertain + Desirable	To Be Drab = Certain + Desirable
To Be Detrimental = Uncertain + Undesirable	To Be Deferred = Certain + Undesirable

Figure 1.2 Assumption Mirror template

To Be Discussed

Discuss and discover pain points that result from mixing vulnerability with uncertainty.*

1. Discover what the Assumption Mirror out-sights say about the Challenge's context.
   - ☐ Play back whether the context opens a Solution Space or a Problem Space.
     - ☐ Solution Space: When your out-sights reveal a history full of *already determined decisions*, you discover that *an existing solution now has a problem.*
       - ☐ Does an existing strategy need reworking? Did current operations over time become *drab*?
       - ☐ Does the Assumption Mirror describe target markets, financial models, and promotional mixes? Do you assume an existing business plan explains these?
       - ☐ What suggests that Client decision-makers were *vulnerable* to weaknesses and threats? What uncertainties did they not anticipate? What impact did those uncertainties have on already implemented solutions?
       - ☐ What obstacles, barriers, or hurdles interrupted how current solutions performed?
     - ☐ Problem Space: When your out-sights reveal a future full of *decisions to be determined*, you discover *a new problem now needs a solution.*
       - ☐ Does a strategy need to be prepared for the first time? Does an opportunity to do something new and better exist?

---

* See Appendix 1 for a Challenge Brief template. Use the template to kick-off a Challenge with a "live case" Client. The template also applies to Challenges inspired by colorful problems at large in your communities. For readability, each chapter references "the Client" as a nonspecific beneficiary of *TBD's* Experiences and Retrospectives.

- ☐ What suggests that Client decision-makers were *vulnerable* to strengths and opportunities? What changes in the external marketplace occurred? What competing products made desirable, uncertain debuts?
- ☐ Does the Assumption Mirror reflect an inadequate business model description? Is there a business model description at all? Does the whole picture seem abstract yet colored with to-be-discovered potential?
- ☐ Play back how the Problem or Solution Space you discovered plays out over time.
  - ☐ The As Is Space: Discuss the Client's current context.
    - ☐ Talk about what leaving things "as is" means. What happens if the Client ignores their context?
    - ☐ Begin a status quo story about the context, The One With an "Old Thing in an Old Way" (Quarles, n.d.). What might happen if the Client chooses inaction?
    - ☐ Describe whether the Assumption Mirror reflects the as is context you discuss. What can you discover from what does not already reflect back from the Assumption Mirror?
  - ☐ The Will Be Space: Discuss the Client's future context.
    - ☐ Talk about what you think will happen at the close of this Challenge. What will happen when a solution resolves the Challenge?
    - ☐ Brag about the aspirational direction of opportunities for impact. What higher purpose or mission-related outcomes could occur?
    - ☐ Describe the details of this will be future. What tactical decisions might lead to desired results?

The context we discovered prepares us to better understand a particularly complex contradiction. Assume every out-sight posted to the Assumption Mirror is true. At the same time, assume every out-sight posted is not true. Accepting that colorful problems lack a right or a wrong answer is one thing. But how can opposing interpretations of truth co-exist in the same space? How might we work with this pain point about our out-sights? How might we use our vulnerability to discover in-sights worth defending?

We'll synthesize this complexity using two concepts: our posture of vulnerability and our points of view.

Experience: Mirroring POVs

To discover our earliest in-sights, let's dive into our Assumption Mirror out-sights. Remember, this first discern phase puts us at the pulse point of the Discover Diamond. Here, we specifically check the pulse of To Be Discovered—the Uncertain + Desirable intersection. Uncertainty and desirability can exist together, and this quadrant helps us see that.

The conflicting relationship challenges our tbds, considering everything that influences context. Context includes "circumstances, background, or environment in which a person, thing, or idea exists or occurs" (Canvs Editorial 2021). To prioritize people in context, we need to discover and discern our points of view (POVs). A POV is an action-oriented statement that tells us what we know about the needs of all people affected by the Challenge. A POV reflects our relentless commitment to serve people's needs. Put differently, a POV reminds us that business as usual comes second to people's needs.

Discern to Synthesize

Dive back into your Chapter 1 Frame. Use Figure 1.3 to mirror in-sights through greater than means less actions.

1. Insert, draw, or otherwise depict a table with three columns.
   - ☐ Label the left column *Truths*.
   - ☐ Label the middle column *Beliefs*.
   - ☐ Label the right column *Decisions*.
2. Sort each To Be Discovered sticky note into a corresponding column.
   - ☐ Use the duplicate or copy function to replicate your original sticky notes.

- ☐ Move each duplicate note into the column that mirrors how you view that assumption.
- ☐ Fit each assumption into only one category.
- ☐ Don't worry about being exact or second-guessing the "right" column for each note.
- ☐ Discern in-sight the Truth column.
  - ☐ Think of truths as what you know or can eventually know with absolute certainty.
    - ☐ Experts would all agree on this truth.
  - ☐ Describe what happens if this assumption were false, incorrect, mistaken, inaccurate, or invalid.
  - ☐ Talk about whether we can verify this assumption.
  - ☐ Brag about potential aspirations to achieve once we remove the barrier of possible untruth.
- ☐ Discern in-sight the Beliefs column.
  - ☐ Think of beliefs as hunches or suspicions that require validation.
    - ☐ You aren't convinced by the evidence, information, or data you currently access.
  - ☐ Describe plausible doubts about this assumption.
  - ☐ Talk about reasons to question this assumption.
  - ☐ Describe contextual clues that motivate us to challenge this assumption.
  - ☐ Describe the possible alternatives that exist when we detach from our personal contexts.
- ☐ Discern in-sight the Decisions column.
  - ☐ Think of decisions as what you are willing to defend based on your evolving truths and beliefs.
    - ☐ Your interpretation adds value to others' thinking by inspiring an original outlook.
  - ☐ Talk about the justification this assumption requires. Describe whether justification brings high value without unreasonable effort.
  - ☐ Brag about what makes this assumption worth defending.
  - ☐ Talk about what makes this assumption dismissible.
  - ☐ Describe whether we could abandon it altogether.

When [context],
I want to [desire]
so I can
[outcome, goal, or impact]
without
[undesirable or
unwanted in-sight].

To shift from as is to will
be in this
[problem or solution] space,
the Client needs a way to
[in-sight] because [in-sight].

TRUTHS
What We Know

BELIEFS
What We Wonder

DECISIONS
What We Can't Decide

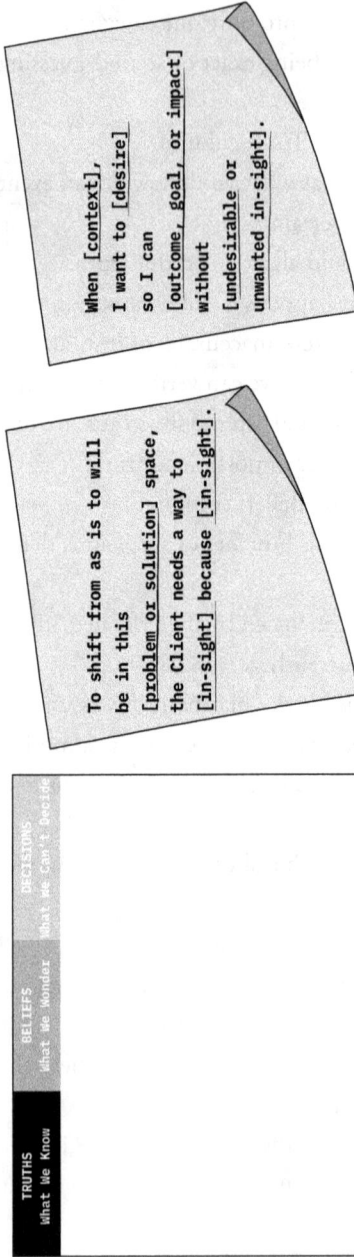

Figure 1.3 Mirroring POVs template: Client POV and Whole Human POV

3. Write two POV statements.
   □ The statements reflect the synthesized in-sights as action-oriented statements.
      □ Use the three columns to inspire your statements. Choose words that represent the "spirit" of the sticky notes and the team's discussion. (Again, don't worry about being exact or second-guessing one "right" way. Wordsmith as needed.)
      □ The first POV prioritizes the Client's perspective.
      □ The second POV prioritizes a whole human at large perspective.
      □ Both statements reflect the context generated in the Assumption Mirror.
      □ Use the templates to structure each POV. Fill in the brackets based on in-sights you discern.
         □ Client POV: To shift from "as is" to "will be" in this [problem or solution] space, the Client needs a way to [actionable in-sight] because [surprising or memorable in-sight].
         □ Whole Human POV: When in [context], I want to [desire or unmet need] so I can [outcome, goal, or impact] without [undesirable, unwanted in-sight].

How do the POVs sound when you play them back? Did the Mad-Lib style approach feel vulnerable and open? Or did those wide-open blanks feel too wide open that you didn't know where to start? Both outcomes prepared you for what comes next.

To Be Discussed

Discuss and discover pulse points that result from mixing vulnerability with uncertainty.

1. Play back your POVs using the three constraints listed.
   □ Start with the Client POV. Then, iterate the discussion with the Whole Human POV.

- ☐ Discuss whether each constraint resonates with the POV. Does the POV reflect the heart of all three?
  - ☐ Each constraint might be explicitly incorporated into the POV. It might be subtle or it might not at all be represented. We can discover more from each possibility.
- ☐ Constraint 1: Desirability Playback
  - ☐ Desirability is all about whole humans' needs. Desirability drives us to discover what people actually want. What outcomes do consumers want to achieve through the Client's product?
  - ☐ What tasks does the consumer need help completing? Does the Client help them to complete these tasks?
  - ☐ What motivates people to identify with or relate to what the Client offers?
  - ☐ What does it take to satisfy people's needs given what we currently know about the Client's context?
  - ☐ How do we know whether people meet their goals because of the Client's product? What else, other than satisfaction, measures success?
- ☐ Constraint 2: Feasibility Playback
  - ☐ Feasibility is all about the technical requirements needed to deliver on desirability expectations. Feasibility drives us to discover the systems and infrastructure needed to materialize desirability.
  - ☐ What systems and infrastructure deliver desirability? What processes occur? What hardware and software do those processes run on?
  - ☐ How does the Client's current technology deliver what people will actually desire? What resources need updates, repairs, or replacements?
  - ☐ How does building for people's desires affect feasibility?
- ☐ Constraint 3: Viability Playback
  - ☐ Viability is all about the current business model. Viability drives us to discover risky scenarios in short- and long-term financial stability. How is the business model equipped to deliver on people's expectations? How did

feasible technology and desirable offerings drive success metrics, like profitability or decreased expenses?

Combined, these three constraints form the "sweet spot of innovation" (Innovation Sweet Spot, n.d.). At their intersection, the Client achieves three outcomes: they deliver solutions that satisfy consumers; they align resources with their unique capabilities; and they sustain long-term success. Win–win–win.

Not so fast on that triple win. Can all three constraints co-exist? That balance stirs doubt, making our POVs act more like *Points of Vulnerability*.

But with our *Posture of Vulnerability*, let's hold a mirror up to discover the barriers preventing balance. Something's missing, and when we reflect back, we will discover which actions move us forward. Look for reflective thinking to validate how much we've already discovered—*even though we are still beginners.*

Reflect: A Vulnerability Retrospective

To be determined in our Chapter 1 Retrospective:

1. First, we'll validate how the Assumption Mirror and POVs reflect our Challenge's context.
2. With that validation, we'll discover how to practice interviews and observations.

If you feel energized by our actions so far, our efforts to use uncertainty as an asset are off to a colorful start.

If you feel confused, keep going. Like a kaleidoscope needs light to reflect colors, we need uncertainty to reflect the vulnerability in our tbds.

Either way, use this Retrospective to discover how uncertainty and vulnerability act together. Our whiteboarding actions probably provoked noticeable vulnerability without discovering noticeable new knowledge. This means we need to discover:

- ☐ How might we validate our actions in problematic contexts through reflective thinking?
- ☐ How might we act with vulnerability to problem-seek a colorful Challenge?

Beginner's Mirror

What's your favorite yoga pose? You know the one. The instructor cues the name, and your heart rate accelerates with excitement. You might love Warrior Two or can't get enough inversions. From Star to Child's Pose, yogis discover new uncertainties every time they roll out their mats. Some days, a headstand happens. On other days, Crow falls flat, a vulnerable attempt reflecting back from the studio mirrors.

Yet what makes yogis of all levels get back on their mats is their practice POV. Every practice is their first practice. They experience every pose, or *posture*, as though it is their first time. The posture always feels like a fresh beginning. It doesn't matter how many times they've practiced Chair. They know just *enough* about the pose's shape. What they know co-exists with the uncertainty surrounding *this* practice of *this* pose.

A practice POV means yogis always feel the vulnerability of what it's like to be a beginner. They practice Beginner's Mind.

Through Beginner's Mind, even non-yogis can reflect back on our kick-off Experiences.

Beginner's Mind refers to an attitude oriented for discovery despite what you think you know. Through Beginner's Mind, we place higher value on the "need for unorthodox ideas" (Finzi, Lipton, and Firth, 2019). Regardless of past experiences, we approach new experiences with a fresh perspective.

Pause at this first pinch point of reflective thinking. How do you feel after the first two Experiences? Any chance your hands got that familiar clammy feeling from the chapter's opening? Did your heart rate pick up, agitated at what felt like whiteboard missteps? Did you wobble your way through, like a yogi shaking in a balancing posture? You might have remembered when you were the new kid surrounded by context everyone else seemed to grasp. Acknowledge the vulnerability you experienced by combining EL and DT for the first time. *By doing something deconstructed.* Or by combining EL and DT for the first time. You too held a mirror up to your Beginner's Mind.

Scratch that. In our reflective thinking context, you held up a Beginner's *Mirror*. In EL and DT, we are all beginners together. It doesn't matter whether you arrive at the Challenge from the solution or the problem space. Or whether the pain points of "as is" made you doubt what "will be." A Beginner's Mirror lets everyone take up uncertain space. With vulnerability as our posture, we all stretch our tbds. Like yoga practice builds muscle memory, a Beginner's Mirror gradually stretches your reflexes. Trust that a *flow* of fresh perspectives will follow.

Look back through your Beginner's Mirror. See how reflective thinking appeared as vulnerability in action.

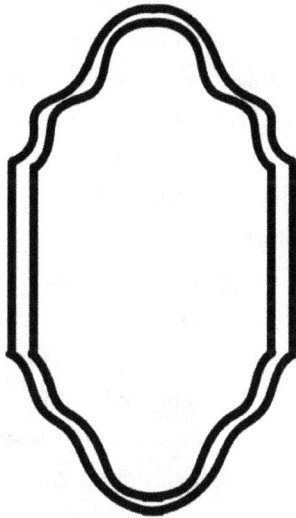

Figure 1.4 Mirror Metaphor: Beginner's mirror

To Be Defogged: Assumption Mirror Retro

How We Diverged

During Assumption Mirroring, we diverged to discover the context of our Challenge. In a flurry of sticky notes, we revealed our personal tbds as assumptions. Each truth, belief, and decision reflected how we perceived our existing knowledge.

Assumption Mirroring got us to debunk our assumptions about assumptions. Before this Experience, we rarely perceived assumptions as valuable, vulnerable perspectives. We saw imperfect information as a source of weakness. We perceived actions influenced by imperfect information would perpetuate that weakness.

Instead, we sought desirable, uncertain contexts as prerequisites for problem-solving. We discovered assumptions about what we knew and needed to know. Assuming a vulnerability posture provided input for the discovery involved in problem-seeking. We generated out-sights that led to three discoveries: our current context, the Client's context, and consumers' contexts.

Pinch Point 1: First Idea Is Not the Best Idea
- ☐ Our individual contexts offered an approachable starting point. Yet, did you notice risks in what you wrote on the sticky notes? Did our personal backgrounds influence us too much? Did *any sticky note* count as an assumption? Did *everything* we discussed sound like fancy guesswork? Did an "anything and everything goes" approach translate into *usable* out-sights? Or did we somehow slip into being messy for the sake of being messy?
- ☐ Some assumptions built on each other. Other assumptions seemed mismatched and contradictory. Others still seemed illogical, wild, or stretched beyond reason. Assumption Mirroring let us take up space with our best guesses and bad ideas. It turned out that brainstorms of bad ideas cleared the way for us to seek clould problems.

Pinch Point 2: No Right and No Wrong
- ☐ Even with no immediate validation in sight, our lack of proof proved valuable. We experienced little to no pressure to overthink because being right was not the goal. We generated our assumptions at each intersection, going on wild and wide detours. As we recognized that divergent thinking and fact-checking clash, our default thinking dulled. We replaced the pressure to look for right and wrong with an empowering state of not knowing yet. Low to no pressure freed us up to further stretch out-sight.

Pinch Point 3: Trust in Co-Design
- ☐ Practicing how we diverged encouraged us to acknowledge co-designers' many perspectives and outlooks. We discussed our

personal assumptions with others who shared different views. We revealed our biases and limitations that, kept unshared, could hinder future decisions. (We'll talk more about bias in Chapter 3.)

☐ We prioritized what we did share: uncertainty. No one judged each other for not yet knowing. We saved our judgment for the problem we sought, not the people who sought it out. Sticky note by sticky note, trust began to reflect back among co-designers.

Out-Sights We Discovered

With so much vulnerability in action, you might feel the pinch of one major discovery. *A discovery about what was missing.* We discovered the need for validation. When we practice reflective thinking, we validate the entire diamond. We reflect on which tbds to invalidate and which ones now help us to defend our decisions.

At the Assumption Mirror's To Be Discovered intersection, we validated valuable assumptions. To make those assumptions usable, let's discover how to validate what we think we discovered.

One way to validate our assumptions is observations. During observations, we immerse our senses in physical and digital spaces. Not just any spaces but those inspired by the context we discovered. In those spaces, we document what we notice to reflect back on what we discovered. We ask how and why our observations validate or invalidate our assumptions.

Discovering observations in retrospect benefits us because we need to seek context *first*. With context identified, we understand where to observe and what to notice. This permits us to focus on how and why we assumed what we did.

After this Retrospective, practice ad hoc observations during future Experiences. Take action through observations whenever you feel vulnerable to not knowing yet. Your Beginner's Mirror will be right there with you.

Reflect back through these constraints. This list aims to validate your future actions to experience TBD Observations:

1. Locate the To Be Discovered assumptions.
   ☐ For each sticky note, think about where the assumption takes place in its specific context.

2. Describe that context.
   ☐ Is the context a physical location? A digital platform or site? A hybrid?
   ☐ If the immediate context is not available, locate an analogous context. An analogous context is a similar environment that "feels like" (Battarbee, Fulton, and Howard, n.d.) the Challenge context you discovered.

3. Immerse in the physical location as available, convenient, and safe.
   ☐ Immersing in a tangible location activates our senses and connects to our emotions.

4. Use digital tools to drop by or login to the context.
   ☐ Observer beware! Video, AI, and other tech-enabled connections complement but do not replace in-person observations.

5. Look for these discoveries during observations.
   ☐ Tasks to be discovered: How did you observe tasks performed? What activities happened in the context? What exchanges or interactions occurred? What did you notice about completed tasks versus those left incomplete?
      ☐ Reflect: "Because [task] happened, I discovered how _____ because _____."
   ☐ Backgrounds to be discovered: How do the backgrounds resonate for people? What characteristics of the background support or deter tasks? What makes the background a distinctive space or setting for tasks to take place?
      ☐ Reflect: "Because [background] included [what], I discovered how _____ because _____."
   ☐ Designs to be discovered: How do existing solutions show up as usable for people? How do the designs resonate for people? For businesses? For the planet? How do existing solutions fail to work for the same people? For businesses? For the planet?
      ☐ Reflect: "Because [designs] shaped [what], I discovered how _____ because _____."

6. Validate the observed Tasks, Backgrounds, and Designs using your five senses.

- ☐ What did a particular task sound like? What did the background smell like? Ask about all the senses that make sense given the environment.
- ☐ Describe as much as possible about the sensory sensations that stand out.
  - ☐ Also consider "sixth senses." Did you detect a sense of time, play, direction, or place?

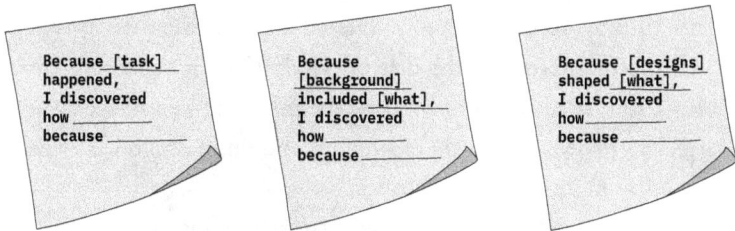

Because [task] happened, I discovered how _____ because _____

Because [background] included [what], I discovered how _____ because _____

Because [designs] shaped [what], I discovered how _____ because _____

Figure 1.5 TBD Observations template

Using observations for reflection and validation is not one-size-fits-all. Observations, like problem-seeking, are quite kaleidoscopic, always something colorful and complex to notice. What matters is that you discover the opportunities to discover what's around you.

TBD Observations deconstruct a complex concept into a ready-to-use shortcut. Apply it whenever and wherever you need to validate your tbds. Bonus: observations start to feel much more like people-watching than a "task" to discover. That's a posture to which we can all hold up a mirror.

To Be Defogged: POV Mirror Retro

How We Discerned

By synthesizing only To Be Discovered assumptions, we mirrored back POV statements. What we didn't know yet enticed us to discover more about how to work with this uncertainty. We didn't quite trust the mix of Desirable and Uncertain. That relationship seemed contradictory and heavy with vulnerability. How could we possibly discern a Client's "will be" future? Could we take the pulse on another Whole Human's desires?

The POVs already point out a pinch in our thinking. On page 13, we began to judge whether the innovation sweet spot was actually that sweet. The balance of desirability, feasibility, and viability seemed vulnerable. Accepting that all three constraints happened at the same time put us in a pinch. Looking back, we remain uncertain about whether these three *alone* mirror our POVs. Do they co-exist? What else would make the POVs usable throughout the Challenge?

Hold up your Beginner's Mirror to this vulnerable pinch, seeing for the first time a problematic order. Desirability was the first constraint. But did that position it as the first priority? When it came to complex problems, did people's desires always come first? Did we first see assumptions related to people? Or, did technology and business models edge out consumers as more desirable priorities?

Even though desirability appeared first, our actions often take it on last. This was despite our best efforts to stay whole human.

Businesses, like the Client, experience this too. When constrained by complex challenges, businesses can't prioritize everything. Per the definition of prioritize, only one constraint can hold the most significance. When viable financials drive feasible infrastructure investments that serve the customer, people feel that pinch. The pinch may not be deliberate but nonetheless an outcome of prioritizing the unsweet spot.

We can be deliberate in how we prioritize desirability. Assume feasibility and viability to be desirable and certain. If we were to categorize this scenario on an Assumption Mirror, we would defer both. Don't take action on what is certain and known. Instead, take space to discover desirability.

To uphold that reflection, use this *TBD* "sweeter spot" reframe, updated for more colorful POVs:

- ☐ Transformative: the Truth we need to act on for the benefit of humanity and planet
- ☐ Better: the Belief or benefit of the doubt that businesses already build purpose into their solutions
- ☐ Desirable: the Decisions we make to serve and defend people as priority

Your POVs benchmark our earliest Experiences and are likely to change throughout the Challenge. Each time you reference your POVs, use Beginner's Mirror to hold you accountable to seeing what you created with a new perspective. Make ad hoc adjustments to reflect what you discover to be transformative, better, and desirable.

In-Sights We Discovered

As our observations validated assumptions, let's discover how interviews validate our POVs. To complement observation data, we can use interviews to discern more about our POVs. As you reflect on the POVs, know that TBD Interviews are always available for you.

Interviews vary by context and POV. A journalist's interview will be different than what a legal team sets out to do. Those analogous, "feels like" examples remind us that all interviews involve at least two people talking about an issue of interest. From our POVs, that issue is the problem we seek to solve.

Interview tone also varies. Some interviews sound like casual chats. Others sound like formal dialogue. Frame interviews to be deliberate chats. When interviews are both intentional and casual, they welcome everyone's whole human perspectives.

Let's reflect back through these constraints about TBD Interviews:

1. Locate the POV statements. Reflect back on the in-sights used to form the statements.
   - ☐ Transformative: What do you need to know about what transformative means in this POV? How do transformative and desirable not only co-exist but also strengthen one another?
   - ☐ Better: What do you need to know about what makes something better? How does better benefit whole humans? How does better occur within what's also transformative?
   - ☐ Desirable: What do you need to know to defend decisions if you were to speak on behalf of other whole humans' needs? How do you stay in service to others' needs?

2. Reflect on who might be knowledgeable about your POVs.
   - [ ] Who *at large* would find your questions appealing? As citizens and consumers, people in general already talk about our world's challenges.
   - [ ] Who, related to the Client, would find your questions appealing? Other internal stakeholders? Stakeholders within the Client's at-large community?
3. Invite people to join interviews with you and your co-designers.
   - [ ] Be purposeful but approachable about having this chat. An interview could intimidate, but a conversational tone builds trust. That trust creates honest responses that strengthen your reflective thinking.
4. Chat with people using these TBD-inspired question openers:
   - [ ] Tell me about a time when you _____:
     - [ ] This opens the chat to exploring a specific time and place, like telling a story.
     - [ ] You could also use "Talk me through a time when you _____" to prompt your conversation partner to describe their stories.
   - [ ] Brag about how you _____:
     - [ ] This opens the chat to tapping into a sense of problem-solving.
     - [ ] It situates people as heroes in their own stories, letting them brag about how they overcame barriers.
     - [ ] You could also use "Boast about how you _____" to prompt your conversation partner to describe their barriers.
   - [ ] Describe what happens when you _____:
     - [ ] This opens the chance to learn about what your chat partner wanted to achieve.
     - [ ] Also listen for outcomes they wanted to avoid.
5. Listen for differences among your chat partners.
   - [ ] What do you discover from what a Client says compared to a person at large?
   - [ ] Do the Client's responses prioritize outcomes that people at large want to achieve? Do they speak about what people want to avoid?

☐ Do people's responses align with what the Client views as transformative, better, and desirable? Where do you see misalignment?

☐ Do descriptions from both types of chats reflect your POVs? What adjustments strengthen your POVs?

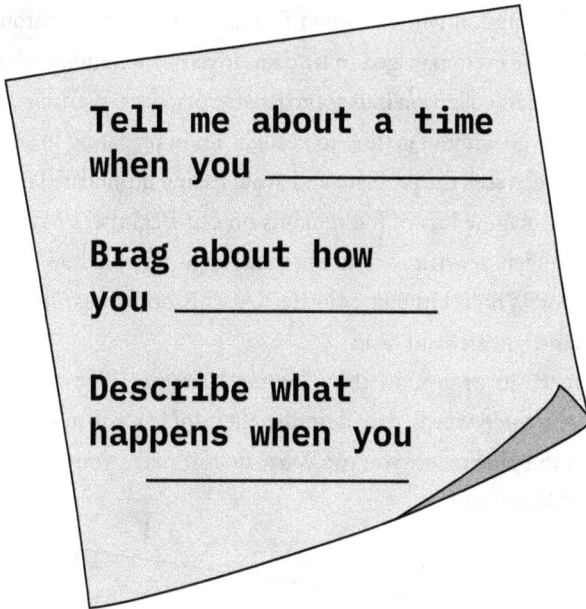

Tell me about a time when you _____

Brag about how you _____

Describe what happens when you _____

Figure 1.6 TBD Interview template

Interviews, like observations, break the one-size-fits-all mold. Tell, Brag, Describe reframes a buttoned-up interview script into a manageable chat.

Like an encouraging chat with a friend, you might walk away with more questions. What we believed to be true about our POVs might turn out to be uncertain.

Our Beginner's Mirror was built for this pinch point. Reflective thinking likely reveals that we believed we understood more about the context than we actually did. In other words, our Beginner's Mirror reflected back an illusion of explanatory depth (Mollick and Mollick 2022). As our hands-on whiteboard actions caught up with our head's blind spots, we validated the limitations of our tbds.

Co-design and iteration defog that illusion. Continue to chat with others about whether they too are in a pinch when it comes to the problematic context. Compare what you learn on-the-go to your evolving POVs.

End With a Start in Mind(set)

From our Assumption Mirror to two POVs, we took action through peak vulnerability. We even managed to be data-driven by reframing observation and interview data collection into approachable practices. We can act on these practices as we go without getting too caught up in preparing to act. We can stay vulnerable to seek the problem and avoid feeling intimidated by research.

Even so, imagine lots of fog remains on our Beginner's Mirror. If you used your finger to write words on that foggy mirror, how would you describe your Whole Human Mindset? At this point, just how pinched are your hands, heart, and head?

Find space in or around the Chapter 1 Frame. Take three minutes to document three words that describe the pinches you're experiencing. What does the pinch alert you to? What does it make your hands notice? Your heart? Your head?

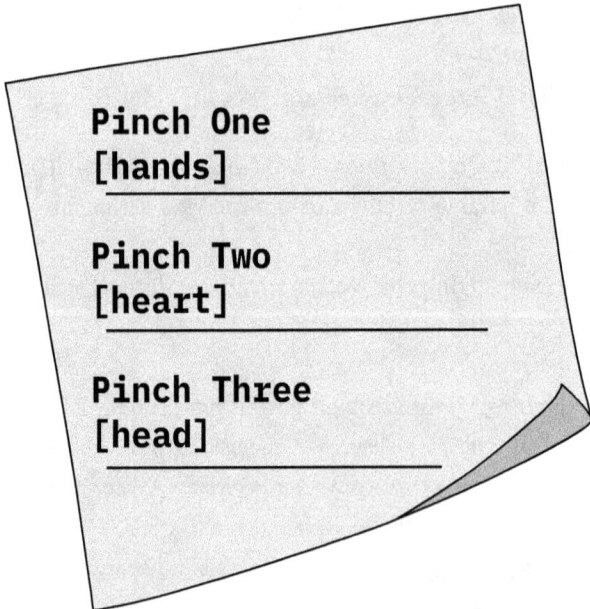

Pinch One
[hands]
_____

Pinch Two
[heart]
_____

Pinch Three
[head]
_____

Figure 1.7 Backcast template

Now, consider how you can reframe those pinches to point you to the diamond edges in future chapters. How will you cast your reflections back into action?

Assumption Mirroring in Business Research

Apply Assumption Mirroring to determine the research problem. This encourages wider perspectives about the circumstances surrounding the opportunity for research.

- ☐ Before naming the core problem, reflect on existing knowledge about the project.
- ☐ How does the Assumption Mirror reflect everyone's preliminary tbds about the project's purpose?

Use Assumption Mirroring as a thought starter to reveal why research is needed.

Uncover decisions about purchasing data, requests for proposals, and DIY (do-it-yourself) research solutions by asking:

- ☐ Why does an opportunity for research exist?
- ☐ How do decision-makers justify their reasoning?
  - ☐ Do they exhibit subject matter expertise?
  - ☐ Do they refer to or review current data? This includes syndicated reports, social listening data, and other historic data.
  - ☐ Is there consensus among decision-makers and researchers?

Answering yes to these questions implies assumptions about the problem may be truths.

- ☐ While truths may be problematic, they do not necessarily reveal an opportunity for primary research.

(*Continued*)

(*Continued*)

Answering no to these questions suggests the problem would benefit from primary data.

☐ Desirable uncertainty *lacks* subject matter expertise, current data, and/or consensus. This lack of knowledge suggests a research opportunity exists. There is more *to be discovered*.

Proceed to list information needs. Pay particular attention to the To Be Discovered quadrant.

☐ What variables relate to the core problem?
☐ What units of analysis are measurable?
☐ What additional context clues influence, inform, or impact the core problem?

Mirroring POVs in Business Research

Apply Mirroring POVs to position the type of problem identified. Verifying the type of problem prepares researchers for decisions about research approaches.

☐ Compare a strategy-oriented approach to the solution space (see pages 6–7). A strategy-oriented approach aims to synthesize specific actions to pivot *existing* tactical decisions. Decision-makers need recommendations for near-term implementation. They want evidence to redirect a particular strategy.

☐ Compare a discovery-oriented approach to the problem space (see pages 6–7). A discovery-oriented approach aims to shape strategic decisions based on broad actions. Decision-makers need evidence about ongoing marketplace dynamics to drive *future* strategies.

Use Mirroring POVs as a thought starter about dynamics in the research industry.

The research industry operates through a range of workflows, roles, and organizations. Writing a Client POV implies a relationship with an external research supplier. This supplier specializes in custom research, syndicated research, or a combination of both.

☐ Adapt the Client POV to describe the perspective of an internal research department.
  ☐ What would change by instead assigning a supplier project to an internal team?
  ☐ What are the benefits of internal research? What are the downsides?

☐ Compare the POV statements, considering the type of research organization.
  ☐ What would external specialists, experts in methods or verticals, bring to the project?
  ☐ What would internal generalists, knowledgeable about the whole client-side business, add?

CHAPTER 2

To Be Defined
With Curiosity

Think of a Challenge that sparked your curiosity. If you could hold a mirror up to that moment, what would reflect back? What would you draw about that moment? What would the "spark" look like? What surrounded you? What were you doing? How did curiosity change what you were doing?

With curiosity as our posture, Chapter 2 introduces us to the Define diamond. This is our second and last problem-seeking diamond. As vulnerability led us to discover assumptions, curiosity will lead us to define questions. Aimed to inspire action, two very specific questions, how and why, get us to define our Challenge.

To Be Defined With Curiosity

Your "spark" moment illustrates a common myth about curiosity. That curiosity shows up like a spark. What happens when that spark dulls? What does that say about your curiosity? We've been taught to look for an intense moment of eager wonder. At that moment, the spark guides us to ask the "right" questions and effectively analyze the answers. We bet on that spark to guide us through what we don't know.

That bet pays off when we interact with clock problems but not with colorful problems. For those, we need something more dependable than a spark.

What Curiosity Means in Think by Design

Diversive curiosity, perceptual curiosity, social curiosity, interest curiosity, specific curiosity, empathetic curiosity—curiosity comes in many variations. Each is a colorful, nuanced take on our practical, everyday perceptions about curiosity.

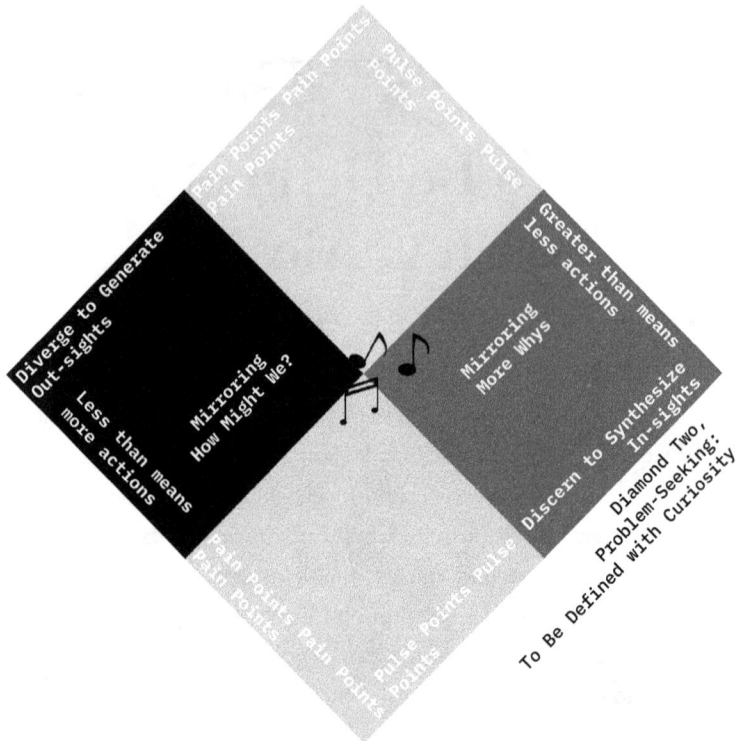

Figure 2.1 Diamond Two: To be defined with curiosity

In the Experiences ahead, curiosity refers to epistemic curiosity. Epistemic curiosity means we want to know more because we naturally want to know why. We already defined epistemology as how we know our truths, beliefs, and defenses. Epistemic curiosity is the drive to dig into those pillars. By seeking dynamic perspectives to define problems, we take a posture of curiosity.

When you engage your epistemic curiosity, you view information as incomplete. It lacks certainty. As we saw with vulnerability, we desire that lack of certainty—not knowing motivates how you act to ask questions informed by a wide range of inputs and sources. These questions influence decisions about how you seek, frame, and eventually solve problems. Workplaces favor epistemic curiosity too. Gino (2018) reports that 92 percent of employees believe curiosity increases motivation, innovation, and high performance.

Colorful benefits like those dim the appeal of an already drab spark myth.

Add a Chapter 2 Frame to your whiteboard's workspace. Within this Frame, let's use Figures 2.2 and 2.3 as templates to practice together.

Experience: Mirroring How Might We (HMW)

A specific question inspires how we will diverge with curiosity.

How might we define the Challenge's problem as an action-oriented question?

So, how might we define a How Might We (HMW) question? A HMW question reframes what we discovered from our Assumption Mirror and POVs. It defines the problem by naming the actions, people, and outcomes involved.

By design, HMWs encourage curiosity because they are open-ended. We framed TBD Interviews with question openers, and that openness extends here. Because we diverge to define HMWs, we dim our own fears about asking one right question with one right answer. Of the people who reported favorable perceptions of curiosity in the workplace, 70 percent also indicate obstacles to "asking more questions at work" (Gino 2018). No wonder we default to asking close-ended questions that lead to drab yes or no answers–*a dead end for curiosity.*

When we decode the HMW acronym, here's what each letter represents:

☐ How evokes variety; how allows for the possibility that many outcomes exist.

☐ Might reads with possibility; might signals a path forward amidst uncertainties.

☐ We announces collaboration; we signals a commitment to co-design.

Diverge to Generate

Back to the whiteboard! Use Figure 2.2 to mirror your out-sights using less than means more actions.

1. Insert, draw, or otherwise depict a table with three columns.
2. Label each column's category.
    ☐ Label the left column *Action*.
    ☐ Label the middle column *People*.
    ☐ Label the right column *Desired Outcome*.
    ☐ Note: This order represents the sequence we'll use to create HMW questions. In To Be Discussed, People precedes Action to improve your reading experience.

3. Add three sticky notes side-by-side above the columns.
   - ☐ From left to right, label each note.
     - ☐ Write "How" on the first note.
     - ☐ Write "Might" on the second note.
     - ☐ Write "We" on the third note.
4. In the People column, use sticky notes to define the people who are relevant to the Challenge.
   - ☐ Diverge out-sight, "If we could sit with these groups of people tomorrow, what would we want to know from their perspectives?"
     - ☐ What unmet needs do they have?
     - ☐ What makes it difficult for them to access what they find valuable? What does the marketplace lack? What barriers do they experience in the marketplace?
     - ☐ How do they distinguish their identities through their surroundings?
     - ☐ How do they use their resources? How do they spend their time? How do they spend their money? Anything they won't invest time or money on?
     - ☐ How do they form attitudes, opinions, and interests?
5. In the Action column, use sticky notes that define the behaviors of who you defined in the People column.
   - ☐ Diverge out-sight, "If we practiced TBD Observations tomorrow, what would we want to notice from the people's perspectives? From their Whole Human POV?"
     - ☐ How do they generally behave to achieve desirable experiences?
     - ☐ How do they interact, encounter, or consume what the Client already offers? How do they interact with competing offerings?
     - ☐ How do barriers alter how people act in the Challenge's context? What obstacles get in the way of satisfying experiences?
     - ☐ How do people work around their dissatisfaction? What nuisances, inconvenience, friction, or issues do they want or need to end?

☐ How do future benefits inspire their actions? What future advantages might they anticipate?

☐ How do people show they are ready for something else? What entices them to stay engaged? What goals do they want to achieve using the Client's product? What goals do they need to achieve?

6. In the Desired Outcome column, use sticky notes that define relevant future impacts.

☐ Diverge out-sight, "If we could show up to support the people and their actions tomorrow, what would we do to help?"

☐ How do they get closer to their aspirations? What would it take to close the gaps between their ideal and actual selves?

☐ What do they want to gain from their interactions with the Client?

☐ What do they need to improve their everyday lives? What could they eliminate from their everyday lives?

ACTION	PEOPLE	DESIRED OUTCOME

Figure 2.2 Mirroring HMW template

To Be Discussed

Discuss and define pain points that result from mixing curiosity with uncertainty.

1. Begin to define HMW questions.

☐ Use one of these templates to play back sticky notes from each category's column into the brackets.

☐ How might we [action] for [people] so that [desired outcome]? (Anderson-Stanier 2022)

☐ How might we [do what action] for [people] in order to achieve [desired outcome]? (Burchell 2022)

2. Play back mixes of Actions, People, and Outcomes that create distinct HMW questions.

☐ Create mixes that express what you believe is true based also on Chapter 1 discoveries. What results when you blend vulnerability with curiosity?

3. Revise what you wrote on the sticky notes as needed.

☐ Make minor edits to hone your intended meaning.

4. Play back your HMWs against your Chapter 1 POVs.

☐ Did the POVs help to define the HMWs?

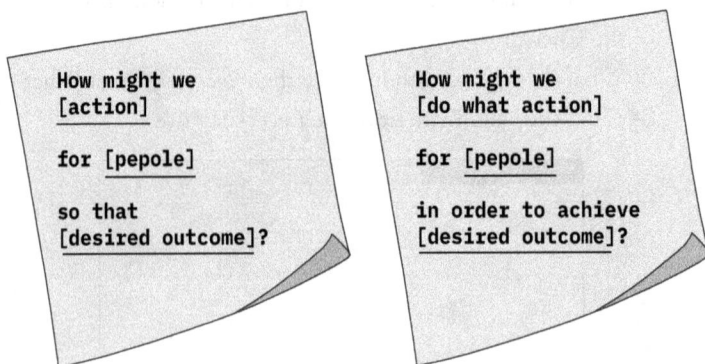

Figure 2.3 Mirroring HMW templates (continued from Fig 2.2)

You may be asking how many HMWs to define. It depends. To diverge with curiosity is to go as wide as possible. That means we deliberately avoid a fixed quantity.

That said, each co-designer working on the whiteboard should aim to generate at least one HMW. Six co-designers total six HMWs. That suggestion accommodates everyone's perspectives and generates variety. It also helps to avoid redundancy. For example, a seventh HMW might duplicate what made one of the first six valuable.

What's most important is to avoid limiting how much you generate. As long as you have options to carry into the next Experience, you're ready to discern one priority HMW.

Experience: Mirroring More Whys

To diverge, we asked how. To discern, we now ask why. In this Experience, we'll ask why on repeat. Doing so will define our colorful problem and conclude our problem-seeking.

This Experience derives from an activity called Five Whys. Originated by Toyota (5 Whys Template, n.d.), Five Whys uncovers hidden causes of real problems by taking an iterative approach. Every time you ask why, you get closer to—on the in-sight of—your ways of knowing.

In this Experience, let's reframe Five Whys to More Whys. That removes the pressure of focusing on five iterations. When we ask more whys, we stand for our curiosity, not a count. Asking more whys more naturally reveals more than meets the mirror's surface.

Why should we approach another three-letter question with outsized curiosity? We could dismiss *why* as a basic question, one that we ask without thinking twice, let alone more than five times. Basic does not mean simple, and it does not mean drab. Mirroring More Whys sharpens our curiosity and adds definition to what we see reflected. We synthesize our HMW options and judge each one for its potential to carry us through the two problem-solving diamonds ahead. At this pulse point, we discern and define one colorful HMW.

Discern to Synthesize

Use Figure 2.4 to mirror in-sights through greater than means less actions.

1. Sketch a rectangle.
   - Draw a line through the middle, creating a top and a bottom.
   - Label the top half HMW and the bottom half Why.
2. Sketch another rectangle that connects to the right side of the first rectangle.
   - Stagger this rectangle so that its top lines up with the middle of the first rectangle.
   - Draw a line through the middle, creating a top and a bottom.
   - Label the top half Due To and the bottom half Why.

3. Sketch additional rectangles, building to the right within the Frame.

  ☐ Stagger the rectangles as you build, lining up the top of the
    new rectangle with the middle of the previous rectangle.

  ☐ Iterate this pattern at least five times.

  ☐ Label the bottom half of the last rectangle as In-sight.

Figure 2.4 Mirroring More Whys template

To Be Discussed

Discuss and define pulse points that result from mixing curiosity with
uncertainty.

1. Write one HMW in the top left box.
2. Ask the first Why about the HMW.
   ☐ Respond as broad as possible with the first Due To reasons.
   ☐ Discuss everyone's first Due To reasons.
   ☐ Document the in-sights that evolve.
3. Use the first Due To reason to inform how you ask Why again.
   ☐ Again, draw or write the latest round of reasons as the
     discussion evolves.
4. Continue to ask Why as you move from left to right.
   ☐ Listen to how you play back more specific due to reasons
     with each Why.

5. Continue to drill down into more Due To reasons by asking additional rounds of Whys.
   ☐ Stop asking why when everyone agrees that no more options add value to the Experience.
   ☐ In other words, when Due To responses turn from colorful to drab, you've hit the deepest level. This is like hitting the certain enough quantity of HMWs.
6. Play back the final Due To reason.
   ☐ Double-check for reasonable efforts to reflect TBD sweeter spot constraints. Can you defend whether this HMW defines future transformative, better, and desirable impact?

Reflect: A Curiosity Retrospective

To be determined in our Chapter 2 Retrospective:

1. First, we'll validate that HMWs and More Whys defined colorful problems.
2. With that validation, we'll define one colorful problem to prioritize during the next two chapters.

Did you notice HMWs on earlier pages? Look back to pages xv, xxxvi, 8, and 13 to see cameo appearances by six HMWs.

Now that we know how to define HMWs, let's start our Chapter 2 Retrospective by defining two more.

☐ How might we act with curiosity to seek and define the priority problem facing our Client?
☐ How might we use our curiosity to seek the desirable uncertainty that evolves our reflective thinking?

With those curious questions, let's dive into this reflective thinking pinch point. While we're at it, let's also turn up the volume.

Musical Mirror

We've discussed favorite colors and yoga poses, but how about favorite songs? Favorite playlists? In retrospect, we practiced Chapter 2 Experiences like we play back our favorite music: looped and on repeat.

When we listen to our favorites back-to-back, we may hear something new during every replay. A less audible lyric now catches our attention. A riff resurfaces and awakens memories. With each repeated listen, we further define our relationship to the music. Its rhythm strikes a chord, pinching us into movement.

In defining HMWs and More Whys, a similar loop occurred. By continuously iterating how and why, your tbds evolved. Epistemic curiosity demanded a genuine commitment to ask the same two questions. How and why delimited what you asked so that you could synthesize deeper meaning within those two constraints. It didn't matter if the differences among responses were subtle. Both constraints helped you define your curiosity.

Turn the volume way up, and let's reflect back at this pinch point to see the outcomes of our problem-seeking.

Figure 2.5 Mirror Metaphor: Musical mirror

To Be Defogged: Mirroring HMW Retro

Musical Mirror: Favorite Playlist

What's the name of your go-to playlist? The one your favorite music platform uses to serve "more of what you like" recommendations? Our preferred playlists often reflect our whole human identities. The collection of songs illustrates a theme that hits hands, hearts, and heads.

The name of this Retro's playlist? *POVibe*. Defining HMWs paralleled defining playlist vibes through the songs you curate. Each HMW acted like a song that mirrored our POVs. We mixed combinations of people, actions, and desired outcomes, testing to see how each stayed on theme with our POVs. Even when we hit shuffle, HMW acted as a constraint, tuned our actions, and mirrored our reflective thinking.

How We Diverged

The HMW Experience turned our vulnerable assumptions into curious questions. We combined and recombined sticky notes to define a variety of HMWs. We embedded new out-sights from our playback discussion into each HMW. It didn't matter how many times we asked and listened to HMW on repeat. We defined a list of curious questions, each one a pain point closer to defining our colorful problem.

When we asked HMWs, we emphasized desirability, or the authentic needs of whole humans. Carrying your POV into HMWs puts your skin—and Whole Human Mindset—in the game. By being curious about people and their needs, we reframed business as usual to center on whole humans. We steered clear of drab financial models or infrastructure performance. We worked with the pain points that came with prioritizing who would benefit when we asked how. We mirrored what people wanted by trusting how as a tool to evoke variety and possibilities. When people's actions and desired outcomes inspired our tbds, we heard a change of tune that defied drab.

Out-Sights We Defined

Within the playlist of HMWs, we defined our Challenge. Our upcoming More Whys Retrospective ultimately guides us to decide on that

Challenge. Ahead of that decision, let's reflect back through these constraints about HMWs. Remember to check for what worked, what didn't work, and how these pinch points move you ahead.

1. Validated Problem-Seeking
   - ☐ The HMWs avoided problem-solving. They did not imply a diagnosis or suggest hunches about possible solutions. If they did, that means we regressed to the To Be Drab quadrant on the Assumption Mirror.
2. Validated by To Be Discovered Assumptions
   - ☐ HMWs incorporate Desirable + Uncertain assumptions. They validate direct connections to what made you first feel vulnerable. Did you use what you learned from the Assumption Mirror when thinking about the HMWs?
3. Based on Broad Out-Sights
   - ☐ Broad HMWs free you to generate more solutions during our next problem-solving Experiences.
4. Validated the Whole Human POV
   - ☐ The HMWs favored desirability over feasibility and viability. They validated opportunities for better decisions and transformative outcomes. Opportunity exists for positive impact.
5. Validated Process Over Product
   - ☐ The HMWs mirrored what people want to achieve through their actions. They defined how people act, regardless of what products they use. This resulted in intangible desired outcomes.
   - ☐ Look for HMWs defined by active processes, not dependent on static products. Whole humans' basic needs remain fundamental over time, regardless of products' dynamic life cycles.
   - ☐ Verbs, not nouns, reflect active processes that result in intangible outcomes. Verbs activate how people behave, not what they consume. Unlike perpetual basic needs, products, typically stated as nouns, become obsolete or irrelevant. HMWs that validate active processes reflect behaviors

that resonate with whole humans' needs. Instead of drab products, these HMWs reflect evergreen behaviors.

6. Validated With, Not for in Co-Design
   - ☐ The HMWs detached processes from your team's responsibilities. On page xxxvi, we defined co-design as how we relate to who we work with as equals. This includes the people reflected in HMWs. Your team creates, supports, builds, tests, and iterates. Compare this to how whole humans interact, navigate, engage, explore, adopt, embrace, and personalize. HMWs ask what actions people take with you. Discard references to actions you take for people.

Chances are the HMW playlist sounds good. You might make whiteboard edits to validate the quality of a few. But overall, you could shuffle the list and enjoy whatever HMW results. They all seem colorful enough to advance into problem-solving.

The HMW mix also comes with uncertainty. When you shuffle a playlist, you don't know what song comes next. Of the HMWs generated, which one defined the Client's problem? This first one? That last one? A remixed version of two combined? Which HMW earned a five-star review, boosting it to the top of the charts as the sought-out problem?

To Be Defogged: More Whys Retro

Musical Mirror: Favorite Song

Now imagine your favorite song, the one track that instantly grips (pinches!) the whole you. Your hands start tapping along. You feel the rhythm invigorating everything around you. You hear the nonstop playback buzzing until it gets stuck in your head.

More Whys transformed an echoed question into an iterative, hands-on practice. Like a song stuck in your head, each replay of Why looked in-sight another perspective. Each Due To reason sharpened the complexities of the Challenge. Within the depths of this arrangement, we discerned the defined problem we sought. Now, in retrospect, we need to decide which problem to solve.

How We Discerned

More Whys boiled down to asking a question about another question. Each why discerned more in-sights about the people, actions, and desired outcomes that defined the HMW. This Experience worked because it delimited our curiosity. It encouraged us to synthesize using only one question.

Synthesizing one HMW at a time, More Whys defined perspectives about the underlying causes that faced the Client. We hit stop on our repeat loop when more reasons lacked new in-sights. In-sights started to sound one note.

More Whys did more than reveal the causes of each HMW. We held a mirror up to every HMW to see which one would define all future problem-solving actions. With our HMWs on full whiteboard display, we tested in-sights to align all co-designers' tbds on one defined problem. In retrospect, we experienced our curiosity like a cautious confidence. We were on to something. We felt a pulse of readiness to play another song, one about solving instead of seeking.

How might we select The One HMW? Each HMW generated could reasonably move the Challenge forward. We observed our POV in each iteration, making each HMW a dependable choice. If More Whys did not uncover anything persuasive about a particular HMW, why not roll the dice on any HMW? By now, doesn't embracing uncertainty seem like a certain enough risk worth taking?

More likely though, each HMW offered different perspectives on the Challenge's complexities. How do we overcome our uncertainty about which one to pick as the priority?

Let's rewind to how More Whys reflected a favorite song on repeat. Like we listen to layers of lyrics, we questioned layers of reasons. In both instances, we seek more than meets the ear. Many repeats make lyrics meaningful, just as many reasons define the heart of each HMW.

By revealing this depth, we transformed our Why song into a deep track. A deep track refers to an under-the-radar song. Deep tracks lack the same commercial success as musicians' other songs. Like a deep track, the reason for the final Why didn't immediately surface top-of-mind. That reason required us to use curiosity to discern and define deeper meaning.

To reveal our deep-track HMW, we had to iterate and listen for lesser-known possibilities. Musicians risk chart-topping hits for below-the-radar songs. We risked certainty to now see stronger validation.

Not every song is cut from the same deep-track vinyl. We need to validate the More Whys iteration that defined the colorful problem we've been seeking.

In-Sights We Defined

Let's validate what we defined using these constraints about your Due To reasoning:

1. Pick one More Whys iteration. Zoom into its final Due To reason.
   □ Validate that the Due To reason mirrors an unexpected twist. Talk about the nonobvious reasons you defined. What surprised you about what you believed to be true? Does this reason stretch beyond a typical or average experience?
      □ Reflect back, "Now we see hidden connections that at first were not obvious but now seem problematic."
   □ Validate that the Due To reason mirrors a memorable breakthrough. Talk about what sticks to your Whole Human Mindset, connecting with another whole human's needs.
      □ Reflect back, "In retrospect, we can relate to the motivations and emotions brought on by the problem. We relate even if we have not personally experienced it." This breakthrough secures an human connection between the HMW and what this reason reflects back.
   □ Validate that the Due To reason mirrors what's doable. Talk about whether the reason inspires action-oriented, practical next steps. Breakthrough covers desirability, and doable covers feasibility and viability.
      □ Reflect back, "In retrospect, we can anticipate opportunities for hands-on, active problem-solving."
2. After reflecting back on the first More Whys, move on to another. Iterate these steps with all More Whys.

3. Discern which reason validates the deepest connection to all three constraints.
   - ☐ Look back at the final Due To reason for each More Whys.
   - ☐ Which one reason includes twists, breakthroughs, and doable actions?
      - ☐ Does this reason also energize your team?
      - ☐ Use drab voting if no clear winner surfaces.
   - ☐ The problem we need to solve during our upcoming Experiences is defined by the HMW associated with that More Whys iteration.

End With a Start in Mind(set)

From asking HMWs to More Whys, we stepped closer to problem-solving actions. Looking back at two whole diamonds, we now see a macro view of how, one defined by curiously asking how might we based on context-driven POVs.

As we next shift to a micro view of who, imagine lots of foggy uncertainty remains on our Musical Mirror. If you used your finger to write words on that foggy mirror, how would you describe your Whole Human Mindset? At this point, just how pinched are your hands, heart, and head?

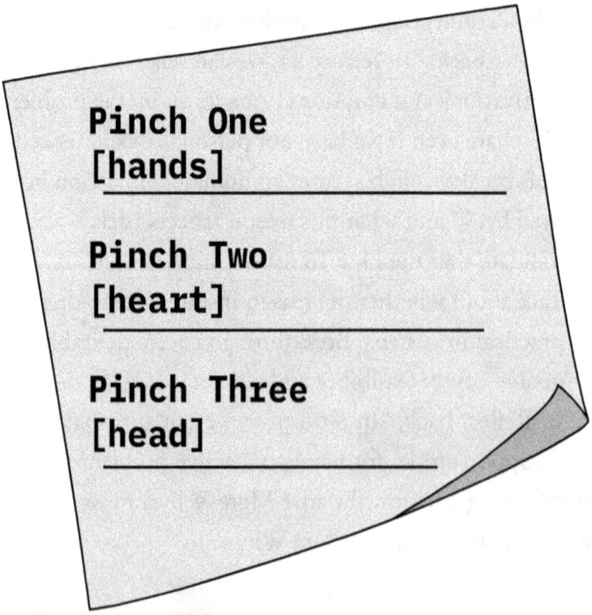

**Pinch One
[hands]**
_____

**Pinch Two
[heart]**
_____

**Pinch Three
[head]**
_____

Figure 2.6 Backcast template

Find space in or around the Chapter 2 Frame. Take three minutes to document three words that describe the pinches you're experiencing. What does the pinch alert you too? What does it make your hands notice? Your heart? Your head?

Now, consider how you can reframe those pinches to point you to the diamond edges in the upcoming problem-solving chapters. How will you cast your reflections back into action?

Mirroring HMW in Business Research

Apply Mirroring HMW as a template to state the core problem as a research question. HMW crystallizes the core problem into an effective question format. It provides a template to create a balanced research question.

- ☐ A research question needs to be broad enough to stay relevant. As marketplace changes occur *during* the research process, a broad research question keeps that relevancy.
- ☐ This question also needs to target specific variables and units of analysis. It defines what needs to be discovered.

Use Mirroring HMW as a thought starter to connect types of studies to relevant types of information.

- ☐ A HMW question integrates actions, people, and desired outcomes. Marketing theories support each of these components.
- ☐ Including people in HMW verifies undiscovered demographic or geographic data. Segmentation studies about current, potential, or lapsed target markets benefit from this data.
- ☐ Including actions in HMW verifies undiscovered psychographic or attitudinal data. Studies about lifestyles and cultural context benefit from this data.
- ☐ Including desired outcomes in HMW verifies the need for behavioral data. Marketing Mix studies benefit from behavioral data. This verifies whether the 4Ps add value to or satisfy people's unmet needs.

More Whys in Business Research

Apply More Whys to decisions about research design. Research design gives structure to ongoing data collection methods.

☐ Compare the objectives of three major research design categories to More Whys output. Match the Whys asked to an appropriate research design.

☐ Exploratory design aims to uncover new ideas and shifts existing perspectives. Decision-makers value exploratory design because it clarifies what's meaningful and develops hypotheses. Exploratory design reduces or eliminates risks associated with unfamiliar environments or insufficient expertise.

    ☐ Which Whys resonate with the objective of exploratory design?

☐ Descriptive design aims to identify patterns among variables of interest. Decision-makers value descriptive design because it supports predictions and tests hypotheses. They often want to quantify the relationships among variables.

    ☐ Which Whys resonate with the objective of descriptive design?

☐ Causal design aims to test cause-and-effect relationships. This requires independent and dependent variables. Decision-makers value causal design because it isolates causation data. This data is statistically more powerful than relationships tested in descriptive design.

    ☐ Which Whys resonate with the objective of causal design?

☐ Look for Whys to match with multiple research design types.

    ☐ As colorful research problems increase in complexity, mixed methods design increases in popularity. Mixed methods design aims to collect data using both qualitative and quantitative techniques.

◻ Discuss how mixed methods add value to the research process through triangulation. How can exploratory whys blend with descriptive whys to address the HMW research question? Without exploratory design, what will remain unknown? Without descriptive design, what will remain unknown? Why might a mix of designs strengthen the whole process?

Use More Whys "Due To" reasons as thought starters that connect research design to research objectives.

◻ Isolate the Due To reasons from the Why questions. Individually, each Due To includes a construct or variable.
  ◻ When viewed collectively, these constructs and variables create a conceptual model.
  ◻ Conceptual models depict the relationships between constructs and variables.
◻ View each Due To as a starting point for a research objective. Research objectives support the core research question. They guide data collection decisions to achieve desired outcomes. Objectives state action-oriented outcomes to questions like:
  ◻ What will data collection achieve?
  ◻ Will it validate Due To reasons?
  ◻ Will it introduce new or unexpected reasons?
    ◻ Articulate research objectives using hypothesis development.
    ◻ Propositions generally articulate outcomes of exploratory research design. Propositions represent broad, unfamiliar relationships.
    ◻ Descriptive hypotheses generally articulate outcomes of descriptive research design. These represent specific, familiar relationships.

CHAPTER 3

To Be Developed With Empathy

Think of a Challenge when you leaned on superstition. If you could hold up a mirror to that scenario, what would reflect back? What would you draw on the whiteboard about that Challenge? Would we see you wearing a lucky jersey to cheer your favorite sports team to victory? Maybe you remember a lucky penny moment before a major test or presentation. From knocking on wood to walking under ladders, superstitions come in many forms. Some represent cultural customs and others create meme-worthy material. Nonetheless, superstitions offer those who believe comfort, reassurance, and control.

Superstitions really hit home for some people. But not for all people. You may place a lot of importance on the symbolism of superstition. Others may see superstition as nothing more than fun and frivolous. They might see it as completely false.

We can likely agree that black cats are to Friday the 13th as superstitions are to uncertainty. Superstitions help people to cope with their fear of not knowing *yet*. They ease tensions so we more easily experience uncertain situations.

How can both the superstitious- and the scientific-minded among us find common ground? Whether you look for heads-up pennies or trust statistical models, we can practice and develop empathy. We can try on others' tbds for size.

In Chapter 3, we enter the first of our two problem-solving diamonds. We'll focus on empathy as our guiding posture. We, as whole humans, are hard-wired for empathy. Our workplaces and business environments, however, lack similar wiring. We need more opportunities to develop empathy, so our next two Experiences put empathy into action.

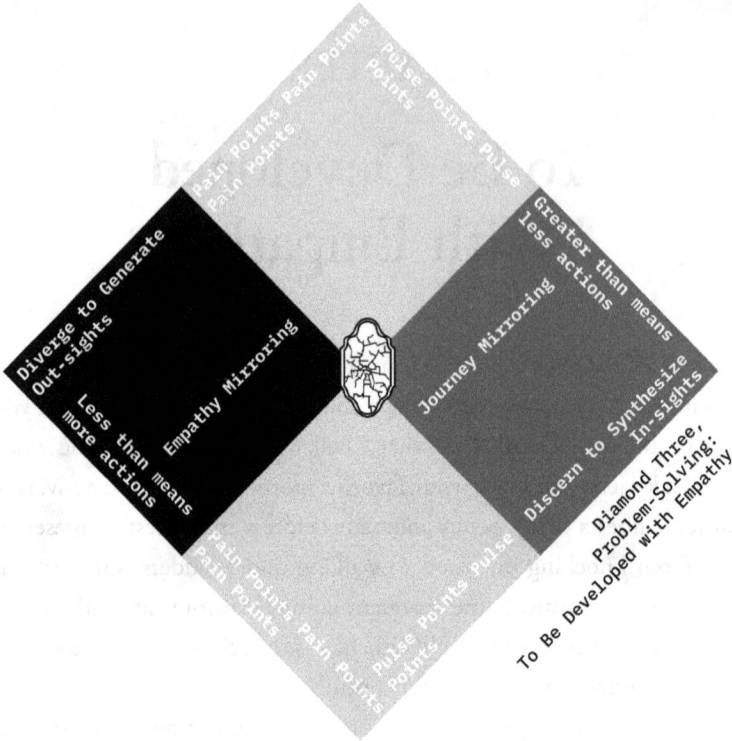

Figure 3.1 Diamond Three: To be developed with empathy

As we'll see in our Chapter 3 Retrospective, we'll reframe empathy in action with a twist. Breaking a superstition together may add more luck than we imagine.

To Be Developed With Empathy

You may equate empathy to walking in another person's shoes. Slip on their shoes, and just like that, you are off to their races in their laces.

As we visualize curiosity with a spark, we often associate empathy with someone else's shoes. Society's widespread acceptance of the shoe comparison offers a starting point to understanding empathy. After all, a love for shoes pervades our consumer culture. A case in point is the sneakerheads segment, driving annual double-digit sales growth (Houston 2023).

But when it comes to walking in other people's shoes, we do not share the same love. The shoe metaphor doesn't explain empathy's downside, including its potential harm (Gambini 2017). People avoid empathy because it can instigate more problems without eliminating others' obstacles. President Barack Obama acknowledged our "empathy deficit," saying "we live in a culture that discourages empathy" (Obama to Graduates: Cultivate Empathy 2006). Losing sight of empathy locks us into a world that spins on the whims of our personal perspectives.

What Empathy Means in Think by Design

Mirrors are to reflective thinking as mirroring is to practicing empathy. Empathy also depends on a system of mirrors. When we observe other people, our brains' mirror neurons imitate—*mirror*—their actions, behaviors, and emotional responses. Mirroring creates vicarious experiences. It leads to a shared understanding with a whole human who has had different experiences—*with a whole human who is not you and holds different tbds.*

In Chapter 3, empathy refers to how we develop our actions based on perspective-taking. Empathy opens our own hands, hearts, and heads to other humans' hands, hearts, and heads. This means we cannot go at empathy alone. Facilitating co-design provides collaborative opportunities to practice empathy. (Remember from page xxxvi that co-design leads to fewer selfies and more ussies.) Workplaces also notice the need for empathy in collaborations. To counter a 48 percent decrease in empathy over the past four decades (Merritt 2017), employers now focus on empathy as "the single biggest management skill needed in today's workplace" (Castrillon 2021).

Empathy, in short, expands the meaning of *TBD* into *together by design.*

Add a Chapter 3 Frame to your whiteboard's workspace. Within this Frame, let's use Figures 3.2 and 3.3 as templates to practice together.

Experience: Empathy Mirroring

Empathy Mirroring meets its match with our Whole Human Mindset. When we see people as whole humans, we generate solutions that resonate with more than their unmet needs. We generate solutions that resonate with their whole identities.

Through Empathy Mirroring, we will develop more understanding of context. In Chapter 1, we began to problem-seek by discovering the Client's context. We also discovered our own tbds. As we now begin to problem-solve, we shift to develop the context of the people defined in our HMW. We'll look across the total experience of people as whole humans. By acknowledging their tbds, we'll develop deeper empathy.

To see this whole picture, we need to look out-sight for pain points unseen by the Client. At first, out-sights may seem irrelevant or too aspirational for everyday business operations. Yet, they lay the groundwork for us to develop solutions.

Diverge to Generate

Whiteboard, take 3! Use Figure 3.2 to mirror out-sights through less than means more actions.

A heads-up as you set up: Refer to your POVs and HMW throughout this Experience.

1. Add a visual of a whole human at the center of the Frame.
   - ☐ Try one or more of these options:
     - ☐ Option 1: Sketch a simple stick figure using the creation tools from the whiteboard's toolbar.
     - ☐ Option 2: Upload an avatar, emoji, photograph, video, or other image-based file.
     - ☐ Option 3: Connect more than one sketch or external image to represent one whole human, like a collage.
       - ☐ A collage can cover your bases in ways the first two options on their own may not. A lot of tbds went into how you discovered the POVs and defined the HMW.

Through a collage, you visualize a more exhaustive reflection of your problem-seeking.

☐ No matter which option you try, take caution not to minimize whole humans. Your visual represents a whole human, albeit miniaturized, with a colorfully nuanced life. We can't simplify whole human complexities into a whiteboard workspace. Be aware of what you include and what you exclude.

☐ Leave plenty of space around the visual's hands, heart, and head.

2. Name your whole human figure *Who*.

☐ Why Who? *Who* abbreviates *whole*. Who is memorable and simple, like a brand name that sticks top-of-mind.

☐ Who naturally transitions us into the micro, everyday context of people's lives. Compare this focus on Who to the macro context how and why established in Chapter 2.

☐ Who also remains inclusive to society's ongoing equality movements for racial and gender equality. Who could be anyone, personifying a wide range of demographics and psychographics.

3. Prepare sticky notes that speak to Who's hands (actions), heart (feelings), and head (thoughts).

☐ Diverge out-sight: Act through Who's first person lens to complete each category's fill-in-the-blank statements.

☐ By diverging out-sight from Who's tbds, you enrich what you develop from their perspective. First person reminds you to focus on Who's tbds.

☐ Place notes around Who's hands that read "I do _____."

☐ Place notes around Who's heart that read "I feel _____."

☐ Place notes around Who's head that read "I think _____."

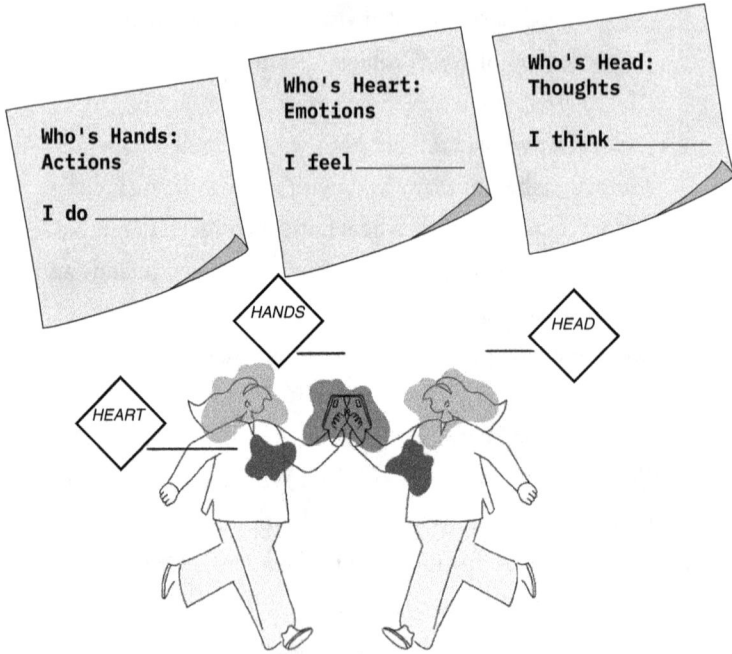

Figure 3.2 Empathy Mirror template

To Be Discussed

Discuss and develop the pain points that result from mixing empathy with uncertainty.

1. Develop a story that details Who in the context of your POV and HMW.
2. Play back Who's Actions:
   - □ Around Who's hands, use sticky notes to develop "I do _____" statements.
   - □ Develop Who's tbds: If I were with Who during everyday moments, what would I notice about their actions?
     - □ What physical activities does Who do?
     - □ How does Who move throughout their everyday life? How do they behave in their surroundings? How do they do the things they do?
     - □ What nonverbal gestures characterize their interactions with the activities they choose?

3. Play back Who's Feelings:
- ☐ Around Who's heart, use sticky notes to develop "I feel _____" statements.
- ☐ Develop Who's tbds: If I were with Who during everyday moments, what would I notice about their feelings?
  - ☐ What emotions reflect back from the physical activities already described? What feelings might their actions have caused? What emotions are evident? What emotions remain hidden, either intentionally or unknowingly?
  - ☐ What emotions carry high energy? Or lack energy altogether? How is energy expressed?
  - ☐ How do emotions change throughout a regular day? An irregular day?
  - ☐ What about a lack or absence of emotion?
4. Play back Who's Thoughts:
- ☐ Around Who's head, use sticky notes to develop, "I think _____" statements.
- ☐ Develop Who's tbds: If I were with Who during everyday moments, what would I notice about their thoughts?
  - ☐ What ideas or patterns run through Who's head? When the "little voice" in their head talks, what does that conversation sound like? How might that inner monologue differ from what they share out loud and say to other people?
  - ☐ What drives Who's rational or routine decision-making? What drives their irrational or impulse decision-making?
  - ☐ What keeps Who up at night? What makes them ruminate on uncontrollable scenarios, obstacles, or other unpleasant experiences?
  - ☐ What gets them up and running? What excites them about uncontrollable scenarios, obstacles, or other unpleasant experiences?
  - ☐ What would they tell a close friend but not share in public or on social media?
  - ☐ What opinions do they hold in disagreement with popular opinion?

Quick poll, on a scale of 1 (Totally Certain) to 5 (Totally Uncertain): how uncertain are you in your decisions about each whole human category? Chances are, some conflict developed within your perceptions of actions, emotions, and thoughts. What one co-designer sees as an emotion passes as a thought for another co-designer. Sorting abstract tbds comes with opposing, inconsistent views. Whose perspective is "right"? Can these categories have "right" outcomes? How would TBD Observations or Interviews resolve some of this conflict?

Contradictions like these remind us that precision does not drive Empathy Mirroring. Expect sticky notes to overlap all three categories. This overlap provides us with valuable out-sight though. It highlights how actions, feelings, and thoughts won't always sync.

We must also consider how people say one thing but do another, making our Empathy Mirror uncertain by design. We want to believe that people's emotions and thoughts drive their actions. External pressures, lack of self-awareness, and unconscious biases only begin to explain the gap between people's intentions and actions. We'll expand on this pain point, iterating on its explanation as a Retrospective pinch point.

This pain point comes with good news though. That moment you recall when you said one thing and did something else? That's you, experiencing empathy in action, now.

Experience: Journey Mirroring

Let's take that empathy in action on the road! Or rather, on the *cross*roads.

The superstitious among us believe that crossroads symbolize luck related to decision-making. You can bet uncertainty waits right at that intersection, demanding a decision. Crossroads offer multiple directions to consider, each with its own set of risks and uncertainties.

Our whole Challenge exists because our Who and our Client reached a crossroad. Or, their relationship will soon reach a crossroad. As Who faces decisions at this crossroad, they acknowledge their unmet needs and step into a problem-solving journey. Empathy allows us to go with them on this journey in a solution-oriented posture. By synthesizing in-sight about how the crossroad developed, we'll develop solutions that prevent future crossroads.

Discern to Synthesize

Use Figure 3.3 to mirror in-sights through greater than means less actions.

1. Insert, draw, or otherwise depict a 3 × 3 table.
   - □ This format develops nine crossroads that Who faces when they interact with the Client's products.
   - □ Each cell represents the crossroads of a moment (column) and a space (row).
2. Discern in-sight the journey's moments:
   - □ The columns mirror three moments in Who's journey. These moments develop into a beginning, middle, and to be determined closing for the journey.
   - □ Label the left column To Be Drawn.
     - □ What would entice Who?
       - □ To begin a journey, Who must be drawn to what the Client offers. Who sees potential value in this relationship.
       - □ At the moment they begin their shared journey, what would attract Who to initiate contact with the Client? How would the Client appeal to Who?
   - □ Label the middle column To Be Devoted.
     - □ What would engage Who?
       - □ During a journey, devoted relationships between Who and the Client may develop.
       - □ What informs Who's decision-making while they consume? What moments show whether needs are being met? Will Who invest more resources (time and money) into this relationship? Will the Client match that investment with added value or a premium experience?
   - □ Label the right column To Be Delighted.

    ☐ What would excite Who?

        ☐ When journeys end, people talk. Who shares their experiences with others. What would encourage Who to share their journey? What interactions would guarantee "surprise and delight," creating meaningful connections? What interactions might "frustrate and annoy" (Miklas 2015), resulting in an inauthentic final impression?

3. Discern in-sight the journey's spaces:

    ☐ The rows mirror three spaces in Who's journey. These shape the exchanges between Who and the Client during each moment of the journey.

    ☐ Label the top row Touch Points.

    ☐ Touch Points are times when Who's needs touch—or intersect—with what the Client offers.

        ☐ Describe when Who encounters the Client and vice versa.

        ☐ Describe decisions that occur at the Touch Point. What indecision may also occur?

    ☐ Label the middle row Actions.

    ☐ Derive actions from the Empathy Mirror.

        ☐ Describe when Who transitions from one task or activity to another.

        ☐ Describe what their actions reveal about their goals. Do their actions also reveal what they want to avoid?

        ☐ Avoid duplicate actions. What occurs during To Be Drawn likely won't occur during To Be Delighted or To Be Devoted.

    ☐ Label the bottom row Turning Point.

    ☐ Turning Points encourage us to gauge how far along Who is to achieving their goals. Did the Turning Points turn *with* Who or *on* Who?

        ☐ What are notable highlights up to this point on the journey? Notable lowlights? What created value for both Who and the Client? When are both satisfied?

CROSSROADS: MOMENTS X SPACES	To BE DRAWN	To BE DEVOTED	To BE DELIGHTED
TOUCH POINTS	I think...		
ACTIONS	I do...		
TURNING POINTS	I feel...		
	BEGINNING	MIDDLE	TBD ENDING

Figure 3.3 Journey Mirror template

To Be Discussed

Discuss and develop pulse points that result from mixing empathy with uncertainty.

1. Develop story-like descriptions within each space (row) at each moment (column) during the journey.
   - □ Here, *TBD* means to be *detailed.*
     - □ Customize each cell of the journey to narrate nine moment × space crossroads.
     - □ Describe each crossroads as if you were telling short stories within a larger story.
       - □ Narrate the many nuances that add up to the whole journey.
     - □ Discern even the most fundamental decisions Who makes in each moment's space.
       - □ Account for what may appear obvious, mundane, or even ordinary. What at first appears to be drab may validate twists, breakthroughs, and doable next steps.
     - □ Use "I" fill-in-the-blank statements to develop the sticky notes, like the Empathy Mirror.

2. Start the journey by asking the play back prompts about To Be Drawn.

3. Play back To Be Drawn × Touch Points:
   □ Discuss the thoughts generated around Who's head space.
   □ Discern how those thoughts interact with the Client's offering at this moment of the journey.
   □ Describe specific features of the Client's products that Who thinks about using.
   □ Describe specific features that may interrupt or somehow disturb Who's use.

4. Play back To Be Drawn × Actions:
   □ Discuss the actions generated around Who's hand space.
   □ Discern how those actions encounter the Client's offering at this moment of the journey.
   □ Describe specific features of the Client's products that Who directly interacts with.
   □ Describe specific features that interrupt Who's interactions.

5. Play back To Be Drawn × Turning Points:
   □ Discuss the emotions generated around Who's heart space. What energizes or excites Who?
   □ Discern how those emotions interact with the Client's offering at this moment of the journey.
   □ Discuss whether this moment met Who's expectations. Is Who satisfied? Unsatisfied?

6. Move right and repeat the play back prompts for To Be Devoted, the middle of Who's journey.

7. Repeat the play back prompts for To Be Delighted. Aim for a cliff-hanger ending. Uncertain journeys develop opportunities that demand solutions.

   □ Note: Use any order that resonates with you. If you want to debunk the traditional three-part story format, go for it.

People develop their aspirational goals within their journey's moments and spaces. Barriers that block how they achieve those goals also develop. In either case, journeys demand extensive energy. Research indicates that people make up to 35,000 decisions daily (Krockow 2018). Sometimes, these decisions impact a journey with minor frustrations. People may respond with a simple pulse check to get back on track. Other times, decisions about longer-lasting obstacles pressurize a journey's pain points. Left unchecked, these pulse and pain points start to sound more like WTF?!?!

Here's permission to drift from *TBD* to another acronym. When it comes to empathy in action, aim to shape people's WTF problems into FTW solutions.

Reflect: An Empathy Retrospective

To be determined in our Chapter 3 Retrospective:

1. First, we'll validate that we've developed a fair portrayal of Who and their journey.
2. Then, we'll validate bias in how we've framed "colorful spaces" to develop future solutions.

Broken Mirror

We've seen how mirrors reveal more than meets the eye. As symbols of reflective thinking, mirrors enhance Challenges with kaleidoscopic color. Mirrors turn drab into diamonds.

This Mirror Metaphor iteration is about to get shaken up. Actually, it's about to get *broken* up.

Look past seven superstitious years of bad luck.

☐ How might we reframe a broken mirror as a tool for practicing empathy?
☐ How might we experience problem-solving breakthroughs with broken mirrors?

Hold a mirror up to yourself. What reflects back? How do you describe your image? What do you notice about your features? How do your actions, emotions, and thoughts show up in the image? No matter how you describe what you see, you describe *yourself*.

As you reflect on our Chapter 3 Experiences, obsess over understanding who you see mirrored back in the Frame. When you hold up a mirror to the developing story, who do you see as the main character? Do the sticky notes describe a core resemblance to you? Does your own context look back at you? Do the actions, emotions, and thoughts look more like you than Who, *who we aim to impact*? Do you see a clear, certain mirror image of you?

No one's at fault for answering yes to one, some, or all of these questions. Main Character Energy, or the state of prioritizing your own happiness as your life's protagonist (Skinner 2022), has become a mainstay of consumer and online culture. Combined with our implicit bias, we may not realize how and when our own main characters creep into the action. All too often, we over-rely on our personal identities in problem-solving. We too experience those everyday pain point moments. We relate to the people wrapped up in the Challenge as whole humans. But it is mission-(*mirror-*) critical to recognize that our actions, emotions, and thoughts do not one to one match anyone else's. Your personal needs and the needs of who you are trying to impact are not identical images of each other. Your *tbd*s differ from their *tbd*s.

Developing solutions with empathy holds us accountable to see many whole humans' reflections. Empathy facilitates how we co-design with people whose reflections are not ours. That means we prioritize *others'* *tbd*s as an indispensable problem-solving resource. That also means empathy boosts actions that uphold inclusivity and diversity.

Break the Mirror. When you see yourself framed in the Chapter 3 Experiences, shatter that connection. We leave untapped empathy on the table when only our own likeness reflects back. Break that "impulse to see oneself as the focal point of the action" (Chayka 2021). Break the illusion that your needs and the needs of Who are exact mirror reflections of each other. Act on your implicit biases instead as motivation to act with someone else's perspectives.

Break the Mirror—a worthy superstition that we get to reframe together.

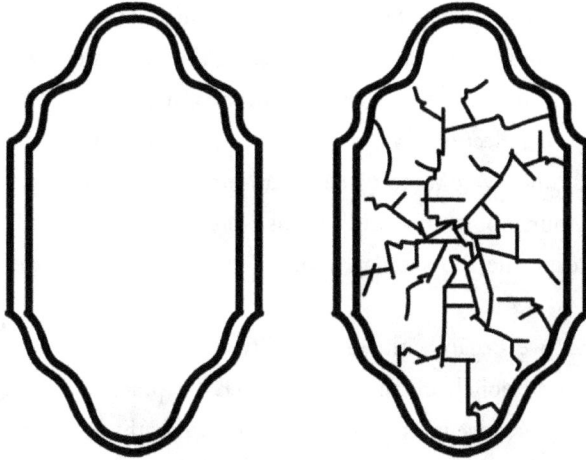

Figure 3.4 Mirror Metaphor: Broken mirror

To Be Defogged: Empathy Mirror Retro

How We Diverged

While we're at it, let's break one more mirror. Broken mirrors help us to see other people, and they can also help us to see other processes.

The DT process usually starts with empathy. But to effectively mix DT with EL, it is more appropriate to place empathy at the halfway point. Practicing empathy as our third posture breaks the mirror image of garden-variety DT.

A keyword search for "design thinking phases" broadcasts pages of websites. Most identify empathy as The First Step. Empathy comes first, nothing uncertain about that. Think of empathy as the main character in DT's life cycle. It humanizes the influence and impact of our decisions and actions for the whole process.

Some DT frameworks replace empathy with words like *noticing, hearing,* or *understanding.* These variations still achieve empathy's primary goal: to reframe our perspectives from the lens of another person. These semantic swaps punctuate how colorful empathy can be. It doesn't matter what we call it or when we act with it. We again see that empathy has outgrown its original monochromatic shoes.

Consultancies with DT specializations start their processes with empathy. Yet, they also encourage adjusting the process to represent the Challenge context. In other words, break the mirror to see each problem for its unique reflection. In our EL context, accepting uncertainty as an asset takes time. Were we to dive in head-first with empathy as our starting point, our problem-solving actions would be less skillful. Expecting empathy expertise too soon may injure the whole impact we want to make.

Instead, we began with vulnerability and curiosity. Both postures broke the traditional mirror image of DT. By practicing vulnerability and curiosity first, we more capably practiced empathy to transition from seeking to solving. During our journeys to this pinch point, we developed more space for empathy in our actions. In retrospect, we see that "Essentially, if you're not able to turn empathy into some sort of action, it becomes harmful" (dschool 2017).

Broken mirrors though? Those are far from being harmful.

Out-Sights We Developed

Let's reflect back through these constraints about our Empathy Mirror's Who.

Out-Sight 1: A Whole Proto Persona
  □ The visual of Who might look more Frankenstein than whole human. Nonetheless, we generated a reasonably concrete reflection of the whole human who anchors our HMW and POVs. We visualized the person who stands to benefit from our solutions. Seeing this Who mentally primed us to put our skin in the problem-solving game. Linking the reflection of a person to the HMW intensified our drive to develop solutions.
  □ Think of Who's Empathy Mirror reflection as a proto persona. A proto persona summarizes our knowledge as a streamlined visual of Who in their whole context. Proto personas "ultimately represent what we think our users are like" (Jacobs 2016).

□ Does the proto persona accumulate as much of your existing knowledge as possible? Or, is the visual more hollow stick figure than empathetic sticky notes? Looking back, what extra "I" statements might add value? If the proto persona looks too streamlined or superficial, add sticky notes to close those gaps.

   □ These gaps may also validate that you need to take action through TBD Observations and/or Interviews. What you learn from those actions may influence how you develop more I statements.

   □ The gaps may also validate the decision to create other Who proto personas. As preferred, iterate the Experience to develop counterparts to your original Who. Remember from page 16: it is okay that our first idea was not our best idea.

Out-Sight 2: Break the Bias

□ As a proto persona, Who showed us more than our usual state of uncertainty. We felt the pinch of implicit bias become explicit.

□ Implicit, or unconscious, bias happens to all of us. We depend on biases as "mental shortcuts that aid decision-making as the brain processes millions of pieces of *information per second*" (Asana 2022). We carry bias in every action, and it is deeply entrenched in our *personal tbds*.

   □ That explanation might relieve some distress about unchecked bias. It validates that we are all decision-makers—we make 35,000 of them a day! When we practice empathetic decision-making, we have a better shot at working around mistaken perceptions of bias.

□ Identify biases that appear in your proto persona(s). Note the list of biases that follows is itself biased. This list won't check for all forms of bias but focuses on what's most relevant for Empathy Mirroring. The quantity of biases listed matters less than how we respond at this pinch point. How willing are we to invalidate what reflects back on the Empathy Mirror?

- ☐ Use whiteboard features to identify out-sights that, in retrospect, act with bias.
  - ☐ Perception bias: I statements perpetuate prevailing stereotypes. When it comes to seeing Who in a target market, we now identify biases in traditional segmentation methods. Demographic segmentation, for example, depends on gender and age. But did we also avoid a reflection of gender bias and ageism?
  - ☐ Anchor bias: I statements over-relied on the first sticky note generated in each category. Instead of diverging, we limited our perspectives too soon.
  - ☐ Status quo bias: I statements maintain life as usual. Look for patterns that lack intensity. Are Who's actions, emotions, or thoughts weak? Aloof or indifferent? This looks like the "meh" emoji at play on a very drab day.
  - ☐ Confirmation bias: I statements confirm our existing tbds while discarding others' conflicting tbds. Out-sights do not stretch to the diamond's left-side edges. No twists or breakthroughs show up. Everything is straightforward and obvious.
  - ☐ Social desirability bias: I statements focus on what makes us look good or what we perceive others want to hear. Look for conflict avoidance to prevent you from revealing current yet incomplete tbds. Don't let the desirability in this one trick you!
- ☐ Adjust the proto persona of Who using perspectives gained from validating the pinch of these biases.
  - ☐ With adjustments, how did Who develop into a more whole person?
  - ☐ Notice whether deeper understanding developed because you allowed the biases to become explicit.

To Be Defogged: Journey Mirror Retro

How We Discerned

Journey Mirroring developed empathy about how we enter, engage, and exit consumption decisions. Within Who's journey, we faced the heart of our colorful problem: neither Who nor the Client experienced satisfying or valuable exchanges. Actions transformed Touch Points into negative Turning Points, splitting their relationship into separate journeys.

If you feel like you journeyed through a funhouse maze of broken mirrors, you are right where you need to be. Welcome to problem-solving. We experienced Journey Mirroring to develop Turning Points in context specific to Who. By validating when and how Who's needs deviate from the benefits of the Client's product, we can identify where to place our solutions.

Direct Journeys

Some phases of the journey developed as direct. A direct journey happened when Who received what they needed from the Client. In-sights revealed no major distractions, frustrations, or irritations. Who achieved what they set out to do at a specific moment and in a specific space. Little to no distance between Who and the Client formed: their crossroads synced. During direct journeys, you might not have realized Turning Points happened.

In general, direct journeys developed positive gains for both Who and the Client. What was undetectable was also desirable. Most of the journey might even look like a non-event all together.

Detoured Journeys

Other journey phases developed as detours. A detour happened when a distance formed between Who's needs and the benefits of the Client's products. Who's experiences detached from what the Client offered. A significant, negative Turning Point occurred, leading to friction and difficulties. A pain point interfered with the outcome of their decisions.

In detoured journeys, the detectable distance was at first undesirable. For proto personas like Who, detours developed into a need to adjust consumption patterns. They might have turned to competing or alternative products to achieve their goals. For the Client, detours developed into opportunities to pursue other development strategies. They might need to develop new market segments or product categories for growth, for example.

Look back at the whole journey. From this whole reflection, we can develop solutions that target when detours occur. How might we develop more direct journeys and reframe detours into valuable exchanges? How might we align the journeys of Who and the Client?

We can develop lots of colorful solutions from detoured journeys. We empathized with the space(s) when the detour(s) distanced Who's needs and the Client's product. It's up to us to fill those spaces with the solutions we develop. This means we use the Journey Mirror to develop solutions based on the space developed by the detour. We solve for the HMW informed by what isn't reflecting back at us, *on what we do not see in that space.*

But these aren't just any spaces. Business conversations widely use the concept white space. White space originates from graphic design. It refers to the blank areas that separate elements or sections on a page. The business world adopted the term to describe opportunities in untapped or under-explored marketplaces. These opportunities validate where space exists to develop future solutions. Identifying white spaces allows us then to fill those spaces with transformative, better, and desirable solutions.

Don't let "white" funhouse fool your reflective thinking though. We often perceive that white appears as colorless, but it is full of color. White combines all visible colors. When we describe something as white, it means all colors of light reflect equally.

Let's reframe white's mistaken identity as a manifestation of all colors combined.

Instead of white spaces, view Journey Mirror detours as *colorful spaces.* As we'll validate next, kaleidoscopic advantages develop when we detour off-road in off-white, colorful spaces.

In-Sights We Developed

1. Let's validate what we developed using these constraints about colorful spaces.

☐ Locate the detoured journey(s) within the Journey Mirror's nine crossroads.

☐ These detours represent the colorful spaces that need colorful solutions.

☐ Use a sticky note or other whiteboard feature to mark where you noticed Who's needs detached from the Client's products.

2. Use the list of color-inspired constraints to identify where descriptions of concrete solutions belong.

☐ Through color symbolism, we'll frame descriptions of solutions inspired by each color's meaning. View each color's meaning as a lens through which you validate possible solutions.

☐ Color symbolism involves how people associate colors with deeper meanings. We develop these meanings through biological, cultural, and personal influences (Skrok 2022). You've already experienced color symbolism. In the preface, we learned about what drab symbolizes.

☐ The colors included account for generally accepted meanings. If your tbds interpret the colors differently, incorporate that perspective!

☐ Which meanings resonate or align with the colorful spaces marked as detours?

☐ Use whiteboard features to note which colors sharpen your in-sights.

☐ Choose multiple colors that help you validate what makes this space desirable for a colorful solution.

☐ Some colors will resonate more than others, so avoid a forced fit between the color and the space.

3. Reflect back: Is the space Red with Passion?

☐ What made Who passionate about their goals at a particular crossroads? How did a particular moment or space inspire their passion to achieve their goals?

☐ What were their expectations? What efforts did they take only to be met with frustration? How did they maintain enthusiasm or devotion?

4. Reflect back: Is the space Orange with Success?
   - ☐ How do the crossroads embody success for what Who wanted to achieve?
   - ☐ In what ways were their expectations met?
   - ☐ In what ways were their expectations exceeded?
   - ☐ In what ways were their expectations not met?

5. Reflect back: Is the space Yellow with Caution?
   - ☐ How did the crossroads cause temporary idling? Was this idling desirable or undesirable?
   - ☐ When did Who need to take breaks? Pauses?
   - ☐ What interruptions deterred or slowed Who's efforts?
   - ☐ How was Who's flow interrupted?

6. Reflect back: Is the space Green with Growth?
   - ☐ How did the crossroads generate new perspectives for Who?
   - ☐ In what ways did the crossroads feel expansive for Who? Did a significant realization offset Who's pain points?

7. Reflect back: Is the space Blue with Trust?
   - ☐ How did the crossroads test Who's trust? Did the crossroads occur with integrity? Did Who feel friction or ease when using product features?

8. Reflect back: Is the space Indigo with Intensity?
   - ☐ Was undue exertion required? How did the experience respect Who's time?
   - ☐ Was the timing well suited for the intensity of Who's efforts?
   - ☐ How long did the crossroads take Who before moving on? How appropriate was the intensity of that duration? Was the duration appropriate given Who's efforts and the time they allocated?

9. Reflect back: Is the space Violet with Connection?
   - ☐ How did the experience connect to Who's emotions?
   - ☐ What connections were low points, or negative experiences? How much pain did Who encounter?
   - ☐ What connections were high points, or positive interactions? How much gain did Who encounter?

10. Zoom out to see which of the detours were validated by the lens of multiple colors.

- ☐ Which colors revealed deeper understanding about the distances formed between Who's needs and the Client's offerings?
- ☐ Which colors validated that Who needed a new journey all together?

11. Validate these colorful spaces against your POVs.
- ☐ Look for alignment between what each color validated and the POVs.
- ☐ You synthesized the POVs during problem-seeking. Now that we are deep into problem-solving, does the POV still resonate? Does it reflect both Who and whole humans at large? Make minor adjustments as needed.

12. Validate the colorful spaces developed against the HMW.
- ☐ Look for alignment between what each color validated and the HMW.
- ☐ You also generated the HMW during problem-seeking. Does it reflect the colorful spaces now validated by Who's journey? Can you imagine possible solutions that fill the colorful spaces and thus solve the HMW?

As needed, use drab voting to narrow your list of colorful spaces. All nine crossroads likely did not develop into colorful spaces. There is no set count of colorful spaces to advance into the final problem-solving Experiences. More spaces developed means more solutions to be delivered. Which one or two points you forward, moving you from this pinch point into the next pain point? Which ones align with our transformative, better, desirable constraints?

The quantity of colorful spaces becomes secondary to the whole pattern that developed. Perhaps one color reflected back many possibilities. Take what developed through that color's reflections into your actions ahead. Colors that didn't develop into as many reflections might not add the same value. Leave those colors behind. Also notice the potential in blending what energized you about multiple colors. Color combinations are welcome.

End With a Start in Mind(set)

Throughout our Empathy and Journey Mirroring, we practiced perspective-taking. Empathy encouraged us to borrow Who's tbds, to relate to their everyday crossroads. We did this more naturally because we first took deliberate time to discover and define our own tbds. Combining Who's tbds with ours meant we mirrored shared experiences. Through a Broken Mirror, we found the good luck of a rainbow reflecting back as colorful spaces.

Even so, imagine lots of fog standing between your Broken Mirror and that rainbow of colorful spaces. If you used your finger to write words on that foggy mirror, how would you describe your Whole Human Mindset? At this point, just how pinched are your hands, heart, and head?

Find space in or around the Chapter 3 Frame. Take three minutes to document three words that describe the pinches you're experiencing. What does the pinch alert you to? What does it make your hands notice? Your heart? Your head?

Now, consider how you can reframe those pinches to point you to the edges of the fourth and final diamond. How will you cast your reflections back into action?

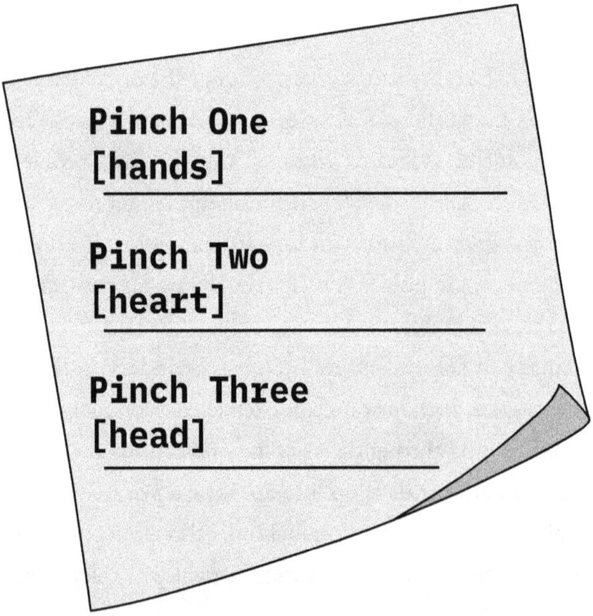

**Pinch One
[hands]**
_____

**Pinch Two
[heart]**
_____

**Pinch Three
[head]**
_____

Figure 3.5 Backcast template

Empathy Mirroring in Business Research

Apply Empathy Mirroring to concepts related to sample design. Possible concepts include sample plans, sample frames, and sampling error.

Before making sample design decisions, reflect on existing knowledge about the target population.

- ☐ Does the Empathy Mirror reflect everyone's tbds about the *current target market*?
- ☐ Or, does it reflect tbds about a *market to target* with future decisions?

The relationship between representative samples and actions to engage those samples involves constraints.

- ☐ Marketers may doubt the effectiveness of "one-size-fits-all" segmentation. Similarly, researchers may doubt the practicality of a general population census. They instead opt to generalize findings from a sample of a target population. This sample enables them to work with time and budget constraints.

Empathy Mirroring humanizes how researchers make decisions about sample design. It reveals opportunities to articulate consumers' identities as whole people, not only demographics.

- ☐ Use Proto Personas (see page 64) to verify if research objectives resonate with people's real needs. Do research objectives speak to what people value?
- ☐ Generating "I do," "I feel," and "I think" statements ground sample design in someone else's needs. This encourages realistic sample design, integrating desirability with feasibility and viability.

(*Continued*)

(Continued)

Use Empathy Mirroring as a thought starter to discuss ethics in research.

Empathy Mirror outputs may involve sensitive circumstances that need intentional ethical considerations. To address such considerations, ESOMAR, Insights Association, and the American Marketing Association issue codes of ethics and standards. These documents outline requirements to protect everyone involved in the research process. Topics include confidentiality, anonymity, vulnerable populations, privacy, and personal identifiable information (PII).

☐ Compare Empathy Mirror actions, feelings, and thoughts to codes of ethics. Based on a whole human perspective, which safeguards protect the sample frame? Are there conflicts or trade-offs between the sample plan and the HMW research question?

☐ Additionally, introduce the role of the institutional review board (IRB). The Empathy Mirror helps to articulate compliant responses about recruitment protocols. IRBs need these responses to approve data collection, analysis, reporting, and storage.

Empathy Mirrors encourage conversations about the role people play in data collection activities. Common names include respondents, participants, informants, and subjects.

☐ What impact does an impersonal name have on the total process?

☐ What name should be used? What should people be called?

Journey Mirroring in Business Research

Apply Journey Mirroring to survey design. Survey design often requires more decision-making than novice researchers imagine. Word choice, question format, and survey length all contribute to reliability and validity.

☐ Before deciding on survey design, reflect on how crossroads impact consumers' individual decision-making. How does the Journey Mirror reflect the lived experience of the sample frame? What product categories appear throughout the journey?

☐ Consider how motivation and involvement influence individual decision-making. Did the journey involve routine decisions? Did it involve limited or extended problem-solving?

☐ Consider how consumption constellations also influence individual decision-making. How do associated products and brands appear in the journey? How do product categories mix to satisfy more consumers' needs? How do direct, immediate, and indirect competitors differentiate value during these experiences?

☐ Linking these concepts to survey design introduces categorical information. Researchers need categorical information to influence measurement scales, which ultimately influence data analysis. Look for these types of categories to emerge across the Journey Mirror:

  ☐ State-of-being information reveals categories including demographic and socioeconomic traits. Secondary data may verify information in this category. This category also applies to screener questions.

(*Continued*)

(*Continued*)

☐ State-of-mind information reveals perceptions about categories that need verification by the sample frame. This category includes information researchers can infer but not directly observe.

☐ State-of-behavior information reveals observable, externally noticeable actions. This category includes information about current or previous behaviors.

☐ State-of-intention information reveals projections about future decisions. This category includes information about likelihoods or possibilities.

Use Journey Mirroring as a thought starter to produce higher-quality categorical survey questions. To resonate with people's whole journeys, write survey questions that:

☐ Include exhaustive response options for nominal, multiple-choice questions. Always give the sample frame access to responses that represent their experiences.

☐ Test conversational word choice used by the sample frame. This keeps survey questions direct, short, and simple. Word choice also builds rapport by avoiding jargon and acronyms.

☐ Drop extra questions to make every remaining question matter. This shows respect for people's time.

☐ Troubleshoot loaded, leading, and double-barreled questions. This reduces biases (see pages 65–66) and eases cognitive load.

CHAPTER 4

To Be Delivered
With Optimism

After breaking a few lucky mirrors, let's look at the light at the end of the kaleidoscope tunnel. To take those mirror fault lines to our finish line, we look to optimism.

Think of a Challenge you faced with optimism. As always, hold up a mirror to that moment. What would reflect back? What would you whiteboard about that moment? What surrounded you? What were you doing? How did optimism change what you were doing? What would the silver lining look like?

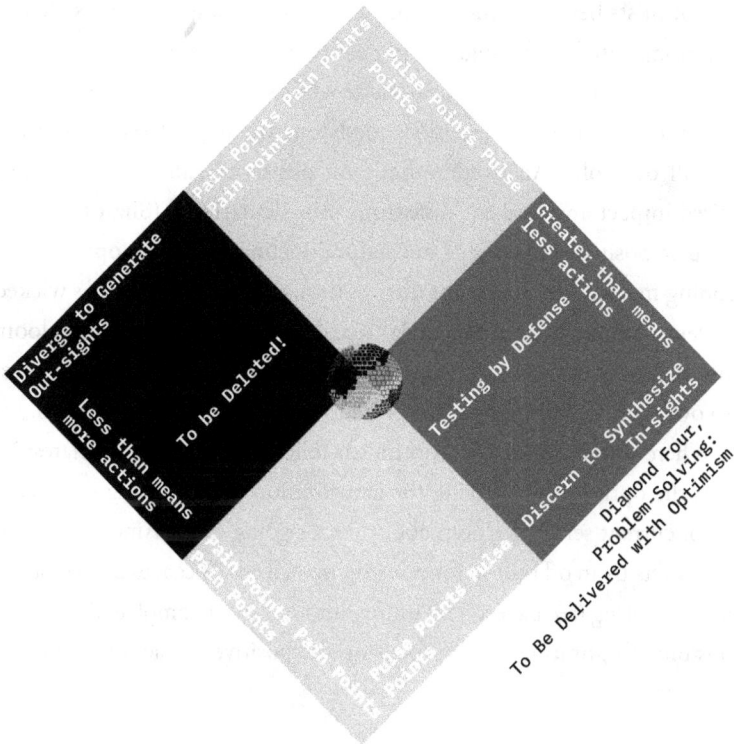

Figure 4.1 Diamond Four: To be delivered with optimism

This chapter details our second problem-solving diamond. We will focus on delivering solutions with optimism. We've debunked myths about curiosity's spark and empathy's shoes. But, during our final actions, embrace a story of silver linings with an optimistic posture. When it comes to solving problems inspired by clouds, silver linings trailed us from the start.

To Be Delivered With Optimism

Optimism appears as a straightforward, welcoming posture. When we compare it to vulnerability, curiosity, and empathy, optimism sounds more approachable. Its natural cheerfulness and warmth deliver a bright counter to many drab realities.

What happens when optimism's good intentions somehow result in a bad impact? We want to actively solve the opportunities that developed in colorful spaces. Still, let's dig into how optimism's signature rose-colored glasses could obstruct the silver-lining solutions.

Optimists beware: a thorny shade of drab can wash those rosy lenses with exaggerated wellbeing. Toxic positivity, or the societal pressure to maintain a relentlessly positive attitude while suppressing authentic negative emotions, reveals the unintended consequences of excessive glass-half-full outlooks. An overemphasis on positivity can undermine our desired impact and lead to "disastrous miscalculations" (Sharot 2011).

Toxic positivity highlights our natural inclination to use optimism as a coping mechanism. Constant distress brought on by our world's wicked problems fatigues society. Our heightened sensitivity to doom and gloom trails our every move—our every swipe, post, and like. Talking ourselves into overt yet artificial optimism protects us from uncertainty's harm.

Where uncertainties exist, optimism follows. Last (2023) declares: "it seems the optimists are driving the actualization and spending that defies the concurrent sense of gloom about what's going on in America." Optimism offers us an off button for nonstop news feeds. It coaxes us to practice critical ignoring (see page xv) by tuning into our most complete tbds. With a posture of optimism, we can focus on the positive impact our solutions aim to deliver.

What Optimism Means in Think by Design

Optimism refers to a posture that believes delegating decisive actions delivers the potential for positive impact. Optimism drives others to imagine the impacts of the solutions *they* implement. Optimism also inspires how others reflect on their own truths, beliefs, and defenses. When we deliver our final solutions, more is at stake than making recommendations. We instill optimism in the Client. When our involvement in the project ends, optimism keeps others energized for action.

With that in mind, optimism empowers us to accept a fixed, overlooked circumstance. Our goal for this chapter is to deliver solutions that mitigate or resolve complexities of our HMW. We are not, however, responsible for implementing the solutions we deliver. Upon delivery, our Client assumes responsibility for implementation.

You might be thinking, "All that action only to hand off the fun part?"

The difference between delivery and implementation understandably provokes dissatisfaction. We are psychologically programed to pursue closure (Joyce 2021). Our minds project certain endings for stories whose conclusion is in a to-be-determined limbo. If *we* don't implement the solutions, how will we know for certain that we solved the Challenge? Will we succumb to "checking a series of boxes without implementing meaningful shifts" (Ackermann 2023)?

By acting with optimism, you inspire others to reframe the value of final deliverables. The solution to be delivered is not an ultimate product but an invitation to continue taking action. You influence others' tbds as they rethink whether a finite solution is the most desirable end goal. Delivery reassigns the opportunity to act because uncertainty continues. Delivering solutions with optimism promotes "a refusal to surrender" (Bergmann 2021). It affirms optimism as a "better, better, never done" posture (Episode 230: Salesforce CFO Emeritus Mark Hawkins's Career is "Better, Better, Never Done" 2021).

Deep down, whole humans believe there is always a better way. Delivering solutions built for perpetual iteration is optimism in action.

Add a Chapter 4 Frame to your whiteboard's workspace. Within this Frame, let's use Figures 4.2 and 4.3 as templates to practice together.

Experiences: To Be Deleted!

In this Experience, we'll generate a concrete list of possible solutions. These solutions will address the colorful spaces developed by the Journey Mirror. At least one of the possible solutions will be delivered, and then, we'll delete the rest.

Diverge to Generate

Here goes, our final Frame! Use Figure 4.2 to mirror your out-sights using less than means more actions.

1. Insert, draw, or otherwise depict four diamonds.
   - ☐ The four diamonds represent one colorful space from the Journey Mirror.
   - ☐ Use a duplicated set of four diamonds for each colorful space you plan to solve for.
   - ☐ For readability, we'll focus on only one set of four diamonds, but iterate as you'd like for more solutions.
2. Label each diamond with a solution category.
   - ☐ The solutions we'll generate will take up the space in and around the diamonds.
   - ☐ Diamond 1: Goods
   - ☐ Diamond 2: Services
   - ☐ Diamond 3: Experiences
   - ☐ Diamond 4: Ideas
   - ☐ These categories represent a standard, high-level breakdown of product types.
3. Write, draw, or depict one possible solution on all four sides of all four diamonds.
   - ☐ Look at the four sides like fill-in-the-blank lines for that category.
   - ☐ Generate at least four solutions per diamond or one solution per side.
   - ☐ As needed, use the pinch points when two diamonds touch to note hybrid solutions. A hybrid solution fits more than one product category.

4. Set a one-minute timer to pace the time you spend with each diamond.
   - ☐ Use the whiteboard's built-in timer.
     - ☐ The timer on your phone or an online digital timer also works.
   - ☐ Once one minute is up, reset the timer and move to another category.
     - ☐ Stay on track with the timer as much as possible.
       - ☐ One minute doesn't need to be exactly 60 seconds but stay in the ballpark of one minute.
       - ☐ Spend approximately five minutes to generate all four diamonds' out-sights.
       - ☐ This includes one minute per diamond plus a buffer between diamonds.
5. Navigate the categories in the order that resonates with you.
   - ☐ If you get stuck with one category, move to another.
   - ☐ Then, return to where you got stuck.
6. Avoid duplicating solutions between categories.
   - ☐ If one solution fits multiple categories, place it in one category.
   - ☐ Except for hybrid solutions listed at pinch points, keep solutions mutually exclusive.
7. Use each diamond to deliver possible solutions that align with the colorful spaces and the diamond's product category.
   - ☐ Diamond One, Goods: Label each side with a concrete solution inspired by the following list of types of goods.
     - ☐ What goods deliver: Think of goods as tangible products. People derive benefits from goods through physical touch.
   - ☐ Diverge out-sight: How might this type of good help Who achieve their goals? How might this type of good help the Client satisfy Who's unmet needs?
     - ☐ Durable or slow-moving consumer goods (SMCG)
     - ☐ Perishable or fast-moving consumer goods (FMCG)
     - ☐ Public goods
     - ☐ Private goods
     - ☐ Luxury goods
     - ☐ Free goods

- ☐ Renewable goods
- ☐ Nonrenewable goods
- ☐ Inferior goods
- ☐ Unsought goods
- ☐ Diamond Two, Services: Label each side with a concrete solution inspired by the following list of types of services.
  - ☐ What services deliver: Think of services as intangible products that vary in consistency. People derive benefits from services when the Client delivers them.
- ☐ Diverge out-sight: How might this type of service help Who achieve their goals? How might this type of service help the Client satisfy Who's unmet needs?
  - ☐ Hospitality
  - ☐ Social and public
  - ☐ Health
  - ☐ Financial
  - ☐ Professional
- ☐ Diamond Three, Experiences: Label each side with a concrete solution inspired by the following list of types of experiences.
  - ☐ What experiences deliver: Think of experiences as activities or events that incorporate goods and services. People benefit from moments that stimulate emotions and social interactions created by experiences.
- ☐ Diverge out-sight: How might this type of experience help Who achieve their goals? How might this type of experience help the Client satisfy Who's unmet needs?
  - ☐ Adventure
  - ☐ Cultural
  - ☐ Informational
  - ☐ Entertainment
  - ☐ Relaxation
  - ☐ Social

- □ Nature
- □ Spiritual
- □ Diamond Four, Ideas: Label each side with a concrete solution inspired by the following list of types of ideas.
  - □ What ideas deliver: Think of ideas as intangible concepts or abstract visions of future goods, services, or experiences. People derive benefits from ideas through their potential value.
- □ Diverge out-sight: How might this type of idea help Who achieve their goals? How might this type of idea help the Client satisfy Who's unmet needs?
  - □ Creative
  - □ Business
  - □ Social
  - □ Educational
  - □ Scientific
  - □ Philosophical
  - □ Technological
  - □ Artistic
  - □ Literary
  - □ Sports
  - □ Culinary
  - □ Travel
  - □ Environmental
  - □ Political

Sixteen sides and three pinch points later, we have a list of possible solutions to be delivered for one colorful space. Optimistically, we see value in all 16 solutions. Let's discuss which one solution from each diamond will inform our final Experience.

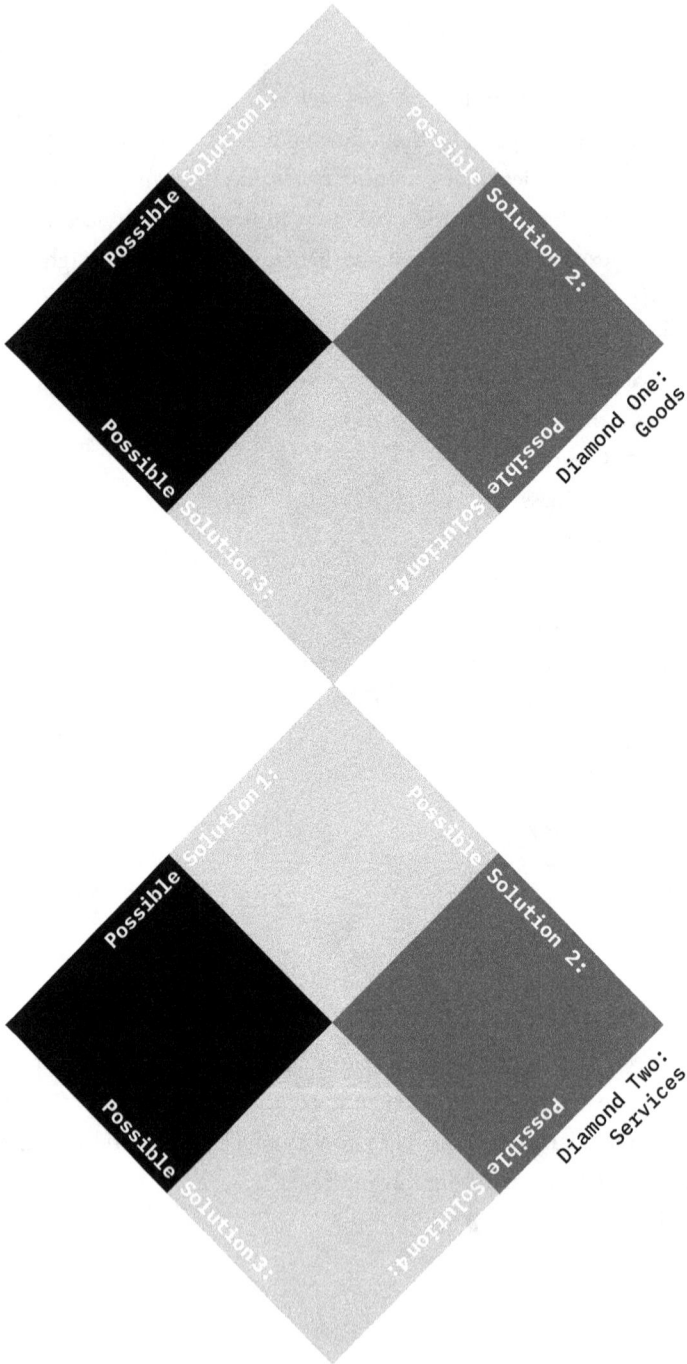

Figure 4.2 To Be Deleted! template

Figure 4.2 (Continued)

To Be Discussed

Play back the pain points that result from mixing optimism with uncertainty.

1. Think of this playback as a critique. In a critique, we optimistically look for solutions with the potential to iterate over time (Blum 2020).
2. Play back the critique questions about each solution.
   - ☐ Use the Empathy and Journey Mirrors to inform your critiques.
   - ☐ Empathy Mirror critique questions: Does this solution account for all three Empathy Mirror constraints? Look for a yes response to all three questions.
     - ☐ Does the solution reflect Who's actions?
     - ☐ Does it reflect Who's emotions?
     - ☐ Does it reflect Who's thoughts?
   - ☐ Journey Mirror critique questions: Does this solution consider all three Journey Mirror phases? Look for a yes response to all three questions:
     - ☐ Does it draw Who into a journey they desire?
     - ☐ Does it engage Who's sense of devotion to achieve their goals?
     - ☐ Does it delight Who and encourage them to share their delight?
   - ☐ The 16 solutions total 16 critiques of each potential option to be delivered.
3. Use drab voting to mirror back your critiques.
   - ☐ A drab vote means the solution does not wholly deliver against the colorful space opportunities. It does not resonate with all Empathy and Journey Mirror constraints. Even when the solution reflects most constraints, one drab vote means the possible solution is not a direct match for the colorful space. That's one too many pain points to risk moving into another detoured journey.
   - ☐ No drab dots mean the solution delivers against the colorful space opportunities. This solution resonates with the whole Chapter 3 Frame.

4. Tally the critiques.
   - ☐ The solution from each category with the fewest drab dots becomes that category's finalist.
   - ☐ This finalist represents its product category in our upcoming Discern Experience.
   - ☐ Elevating one finalist per category signals that this solution is worth defending.
5. Delete all other drab solutions.
   - ☐ Take "delete" to be literal or figurative.
     - ☐ Use the whiteboard delete function or sketch an X over drab solutions.
6. Repeat the critiques as needed if a tie within a category occurs.
   - ☐ Drab vote between the tied solutions until one earns the more favorable critique.

Editing by deleting might seem counterintuitive, yet we can't overlook its impact. Deleting 12 solutions eliminates longer-term, riskier alternatives that won't be delivered. How optimistic does the act of deleting actually feel? An edited list delivers the message that we won't defend just anything. These finalists position us to deliver one optimistic solution to the HMW question.

We are uncertain about which finalists will ultimately be delivered. Will it be a service? An idea? A hybrid? Yet, we have optimistic choices to carry forward into the last Experience.

Experience: Testing by Defense

Who knew how optimistic the act of deleting might feel? We matched colorful spaces to solutions with the greatest potential for impact. But what we couldn't completely delete was our uncertainty. We are not sure how to deliver descriptions of the finalists' future impacts.

To deliver solutions we can defend, we need to put all four finalists to the test. Meet Testing by Defense, a look in-sight of the four possible solutions to be delivered.

In this Experience, you'll test each finalist by discerning the impact of future actions. What will happen when the Client implements the solution? How might we embed optimism for future implementation in what we deliver?

Like we want all cloud problems to show their silver linings, we want all four finalists to pass this test. If all four pass, we deliver all four to the Client. That solution set gives the Client agency to decide how to optimistically move ahead.

At the same time, "fact-based optimism" (Mau 2020) gets us to prioritize which solutions to defend. We take responsibility to defend the type of impact the solution will likely have. We are accountable for the impact on the Client, Who, and shared communities at large.

We are less uncertain about solving our colorful problem because we can visualize four solutions. But, what about the impact of these finalists? How might we test each solution to learn if its impact is worth defending?

Discern to Synthesize

Use Figure 4.3 to mirror in-sights through greater than means less actions.

1. Begin with a 2 × 2 grid.
   - Label the X-axis *Deliberate.*
     - Label the endpoints as Not Deliberate (far left) to Deliberate (far right).
     - This continuum ranges from "We do not intend to make this impact" to "This is the impact we intend to make."
   - Label the Y-axis *Desirability.*
     - Label the endpoints as Not Desirable (bottom) to Desirable (top).
     - This continuum ranges from "We will impact other problems including injury, damage, or harm" to "We would impact extra benefits or premium value."
2. Make three copies of the blank template, one for each of the four finalists.
   - Label each template as a finalist's category: Good, Service, Experience, and Idea.

3. Start with one finalist.
- ☐ Synthesize descriptions of the finalist's impact if the Client were to take further action.
  - ☐ Discern in-sight the Desirable × Deliberate intersection.
    - ☐ How does Who experience satisfaction because of the solution? How does the solution meet their expectations? What does the solution achieve on their behalf? What's the best thing about this impact? What progress occurs?
    - ☐ Does the Client POV align with these in-sights? Does the Whole Human POV align with these in-sights?
  - ☐ Discern in-sight the Desirable × Not Deliberate intersection.
    - ☐ How does Who's experience with the solution exceed their expectations? What does Who learn, realize, or acknowledge because of the solution's impact? How does this impact surprise Who in nonobvious ways? Does the impact connect to Who's emotions in a uniquely positive way?
    - ☐ Does the Client POV align with these in-sights? Does the Whole Human POV align with these in-sights?
  - ☐ Discern in-sight the Not Desirable × Deliberate intersection.
    - ☐ How does Who's experience distance them from their original needs? How does this change their journey in a uniquely negative way? What about their actions, emotions, and thoughts throughout the journey? What unanticipated trade-offs must now be prioritized?
    - ☐ Does the Client POV align with these in-sights? Does the Whole Human POV align with these in-sights?
  - ☐ Discern in-sight the Not Desirable × Not Deliberate intersection.
    - ☐ How does Who's experience with the solution introduce barriers, obstacles, or hurdles? How does the solution's impact become its own problem? Does it add unsought or unwanted burdens to Who's experience?
    - ☐ Does the Client POV align with these in-sights? Does the Whole Human POV align with these in-sights?

4. Iterate these steps with the three remaining finalists.
   - ☐ Using our synthesized in-sights about all four finalists, what decisions now face us ahead of delivery?
     - ☐ *Should* we deliver each solution?
     - ☐ *Could* we deliver each solution?
     - ☐ Most importantly, *will* we deliver each solution?

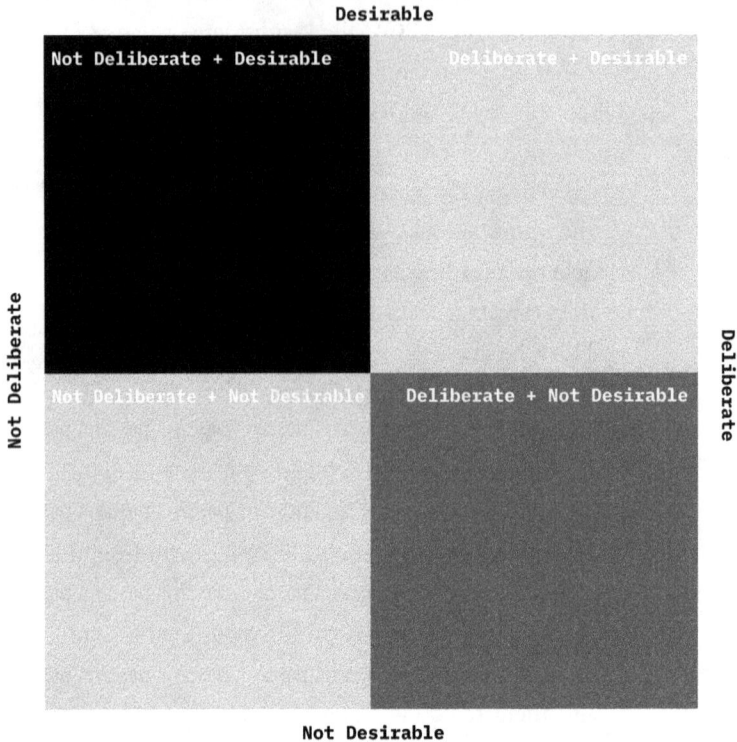

Figure 4.3 Testing by Defense template

To Be Discussed

Play back pulse points that result from mixing optimism with uncertainty.

1. Play back your Testing by Defense in-sights using color symbolism. This iteration may feel like the Journey Mirror Retro.
   - ☐ Use each color's meaning as a lens to examine the solution's consequences. Look for risks to head-off when you hand-off your solution(s) during delivery.

- ☐ Iterate the playback with all four finalists.
- ☐ Add sticky notes as you go, helping you to defend what to deliver or to delete.

2. Play back for Red, or In-sights about the Regulatory or Legal context:
   - ☐ How does the finalist interact with legislative requirements? Do Who and our Client appear protected for fair, just business practices?
   - ☐ Would legal redlines create barriers or pain points?

3. Play back for Orange, or In-sights about the Social context:
   - ☐ How does this finalist interact with health and well-being? How does this finalist uphold or improve psychological and physical wellness?
   - ☐ Would this finalist lead to an orange alert, like those issued for air quality concerns?

4. Play back for Yellow, or In-sights about the Cultural context:
   - ☐ How does this finalist interact with the demographic characteristics of the community and society?
   - ☐ How does this finalist reflect current cultural norms and dynamic movements?

5. Play back for Green, or In-sights about Natural Environment context:
   - ☐ How does this finalist interact with our natural resources?
   - ☐ How does this finalist avoid contributing to the global climate crisis?
   - ☐ Would Mother Earth green-light this finalist?

6. Play back for Blue, or In-sights about Technology:
   - ☐ How does this finalist interact with the digital and virtual landscape?
   - ☐ How does this finalist uphold ethical, humane use of advances in artificial intelligence?
   - ☐ Would this finalist live up to blue's reputation as "people's favorite color choice"?
   - ☐ Would it compare to or inspire a blue logo similar to big tech brands' logos?

7. Play back for Indigo, or In-sights about Competition:
   - ☐ How does this finalist interact with competitive factors?
   - ☐ How do you describe entry, power of buyers and suppliers, and existing substitutes?

8. Play back for Violet, or In-sights about Politics:
   □ How does this finalist interact with government policies?
   □ What political motivations might undermine its impact?
   □ Would bipartisanship be possible, when blue and red mix?

Reflect: An Optimism Retrospective

To be determined in the Chapter 4 Retrospective:

1. First, we'll validate how To Be Deleted! and Testing by Defense revealed a set of to be delivered solutions.
2. Then, we'll validate how low-fidelity (lo-fi) prototypes add value to an optimistically uncertain deliverable.

During our Chapter 4 Retrospective, challenge yourself to *take it all in*. Look at the whole picture reflected back from all four Frames. Bring your most complete tbds to what lies ahead. Use Beginner's Mirror to look at each finalist as though you've never seen it before. See solutions with vulnerability. Use Musical Mirror to iterate on repeat and play favorites. See solutions with curiosity. Use Broken Mirror to sideline your needs. See solutions with empathy.

   □ How might we act with optimism and deliver a validated
     solution or solution set?
   □ How might we hand-off optimism during delivery and ahead
     of implementation?

This final moment of reflective thinking deserves a celebration. It needs a Mirror Metaphor that spans the whole reflection of all our reflective thinking.

A look into our metaphorical kaleidoscope's viewfinder reflects another colorful symbol. It turns out a celebratory symbol evolved when we weren't looking for it.

Let's follow the call of the disco ball.

Disco Ball Mirror

The goal of our final Mirror Metaphor is to round out your Experiences—figuratively and literally. To *round out*, we will *round up* our whole practice.

Connect every frame and reframe of every Experience. Connect the pain points from all the out-sights generated. Connect the pulse points from all the in-sights synthesized. Connect the pinch points when reflective thinking validated your tbds with ongoing uncertainty. Connect every colorful sticky note in every colorful diamond, each a mirror image of your actions.

When collected, these connections add up to resemble a disco ball. Your reflections wrap around your actions like diamond-shaped mirrors wrap around a disco ball. Pause to acknowledge that none of these reflections existed before you dove into EL and DT. In the Preface, we committed to "celebrate the uncertainty in our world's colorful problems." Now's the time to celebrate how you delivered this disco ball from scratch.

Disco balls, like kaleidoscopes, use mirrors to cast new light and frame sensory experiences. When light catches a disco ball's mirrors, confetti-like spots and dots of light take up the surrounding space. Disco balls exude playfulness and "wickedly good" vibes. We need positive counters like those to put wicked Challenges into perspective.

This Retrospective puts a spin on the history of the disco ball. Also known as mirror balls, disco balls first lit up pop culture in the 1920s and found their groove in the 1970s. Nightclubs needed an atmosphere to attract guests but lacked cash flow. Club owners decided to experiment with shining light onto a sphere. As a result, glittering light eliminated unwanted drab space. Disco balls solved an undesirable Turning Point by delivering movement and ambiance. They filled what we know as a colorful space with color. Decades later, the disco ball still offers a low-cost, low-tech way to connect people and fill spaces with beauty. Disco balls validate that even solutions that appear as bare minimums can flood a Challenge with optimism.

Social media trends and an official emoji keep the disco ball relevant. People desire the aliveness and energy associated with disco balls. They appreciate disco balls as go-to favorites of function, freedom, and fun (Picard 2022).

We can also look to disco balls for a history lesson in fidelity. Think of fidelity as the degree of exactness conveyed by a solution. High fidelity describes a solution that closely matches the look and feel of a final product. Low fidelity describes a solution at its bare minimum. There's more about fidelity ahead but reflect on this: disco balls delivered low fidelity with high impact. Disco balls show that solutions with a bare minimum "look and feel" can light up a Challenge and deliver optimism.

As you reflect back on your solutions to be delivered, use the disco ball as a metaphor for low fidelity. What appears as rough around the edges or not fully formed can continue to spin with optimism.

Now, it's your turn to celebrate.

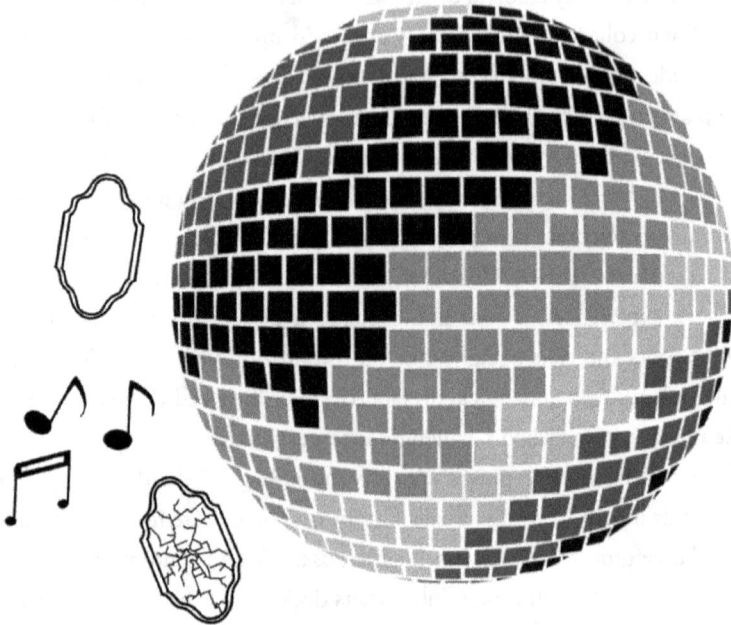

Figure 4.4 Mirror Metaphor: Disco ball mirror

To Be Defogged: To Be Deleted! Retro

How We Diverged

Looking back at To Be Deleted!, the four product category diamonds may now resemble the shape of our Double Double Diamond model. But, did you notice To Be Deleted! included two constraints not seen in other Experiences?

To Be Deleted! was the first Experience to involve setting a timer. It was also the first Experience to name a specific quantity to generate as you diverged. Optimistically, you were too caught up with optimism to notice these unfamiliar constraints. Yet, the impact of those two constraints quickly added up. *Emphasis on quick.*

By setting a one-minute timer, you experienced the pace of a design sprint. Look back to page xxxii. There, we described sprints as outcome-oriented ways "to make really great progress on a challenge in a relatively short amount of time" ("How to Use Sprints to Work Smart and Upskill" 2022). A preset timer moved you from one diamond to another. This "time-boxed condition" ("What Are Design Sprints? | IxDF" 2020) introduced a constraint that tested your ability to act with conflicting circumstances. Limiting how you diverged to 60-second bursts required you to go wide yet fast. Sprints thrive with speed. Time delimited your actions but generated higher-quality output.

In retrospect, you can now reframe all previous Experiences with divergent thinking as *unsprints* (Beran 2022). We needed to first *unsprint* with uncertainty, not bulldoze our way into it. Unsprints deliberately inserted drag into our actions. Over time, we built muscle memory around our diverge, discern, and reflect pattern. Our ways of knowing became more reflective and less uncertain. That freed our Whole Human Mindset to take quick actions that added up.

With the timer set, we focused on a specific quantity. By sprinting among product categories, we delivered a list of 16 solutions. But why did we generate such an exact number, only to discard what excited us? Did our sprint result more so in what we did not deliver? What can we learn from the pinch of relegating 12 solutions into digital garbage?

Deleting gets a bad rap. We even symbolize the delete button as a trash can, further perpetuating its drab reputation. When we reframe deleting as *deliberate editing*, we enhance how we deliver solutions. We get to be deliberate in defense of what makes each diamond's solution better. Deliberate editing means the colorful spaces fill up with transformative solutions.

Out-Sights We Delivered

Let's reflect back through these constraints to validate the pinch of reflective thinking experienced during To Be Deleted!.

1. Zoom into each finalist.
   - ☐ After validating how you edited the first finalist, move to the next finalist.
   - ☐ Iterate these actions for each finalist.

2. Reflect back: Is this solution edited for should?
   - ☐ Interpret "should" as *must* or *obligated.*
     - ☐ Should suggests both a higher level of certainty and a lack of options. Should, therefore, defies how we use desirable uncertainty as an asset for decision-making.
   - ☐ When it comes to this solution, we wish _____.
     - ☐ What improvements need to happen to add features or utilities?
     - ☐ What difference should those improvements make on your uncertainty?
   - ☐ To validate should, respond to *Should we deliver this solution?*
3. Reflect back: Is this solution edited for could?
   - ☐ Interpret "could" as *potentially will.* Unlike should, could optimistically tempts us with implied potential.
     - ☐ Could suggests an innate willingness to take solution-oriented actions.
   - ☐ When it comes to this solution, we wonder _____.
     - ☐ What questions remain unanswered?
     - ☐ What uncertainties still exist about how this solution might work?
   - ☐ To validate could, respond to *Could we deliver this solution?*
4. Reflect back: Is this finalist edited for will?
   - ☐ Interpret "will" as a *choice* to take action and reach a decision.
     - ☐ When we edit for will, we validate a pinch point more powerful than our "should wish" and "could wonder." Identifying *worry* in will drives us to deliver the most actionable solutions based on our most complete reflective thinking process. Where there's a will, there's a worry.
   - ☐ When it comes to this solution, we worry _____.
     - ☐ What do you find difficult about this solution? What drawbacks exist? How does this solution test your tbds?
     - ☐ What do you find likable or easy that it might be too good to be true?
   - ☐ To validate will, respond to *Will we deliver this solution?*

5. Reflect back on which finalist(s) deliver the most worry to you.
   ☐ Which finalist(s) stretch our criteria for transformative, better, and desirable impact? Are all three criteria represented?
   ☐ Which solution still energizes everyone because it still needs deeper understanding? Is some desirable uncertainty still at play? Does this solution involve twists, breakthroughs, and doable actions?
6. Delete—deliberately edit—solutions that did not sufficiently worry you.
   ☐ Draw an X, move to trash, scratch out, or otherwise symbolize that finalist(s) without worry are no longer finalists.
7. Keep only the finalists that deliver worry.
   ☐ Worry gives us a chance to reflect more deeply about what will be delivered.
   ☐ A lack of worry suggests we aren't wholly invested. *Whole humans worry.*

Optimism and worry may not intuitively go hand-in-hand. Yet, a posture of optimism fuels how we deliver a process-oriented solution. Optimism implies that ongoing improvements come with the delivery. Where there's the uncertainty of worry, there's an optimistic will to deliver.

How does the final edit look in retrospect? How many solutions carry into the final Retrospective? How did it feel to deliberately edit for fewer, better solutions?

You put your worry to work, which meant your optimism was at play. That's worthy of a disco ball celebration!

To Be Defogged: Testing by Defense Retro

You tested the impacts of each finalist solution. You worried your way into delivering an edited solution list. Only one Retrospective remains ahead of delivery. We want to deliver a high-quality solution, one that represents our most complete, plausible, and compelling ways of knowing based on everything we've experienced.

In this final Retrospective, we'll iterate three familiar questions. We've reflected on whether we should, could, or will deliver. Swap deliver for defend and apply these modified questions to validate the edited finalist list.

Should you *defend* this solution?
Could you *defend* this solution?
Will you *defend* this solution?

How We Discerned

Testing by Defense put how we discerned to the test. We looked for blind spots in our mirrors, testing for pulse points as we synthesized. This resulted in the tightest, most deliberate edit of solutions.

Testing by Defense also parallels the sprint-like actions from To Be Deleted!. Near the end of design sprints, a testing phase refines solutions for delivery. Testing uncovers potential flaws or issues and holds buffer time to adjust actions. By testing what happened when we "purposefully insert friction" (Katz 2020), we vetted uncertain scenarios and revealed risks *before* implementation. This safeguarded the Client from future exertion on anything but solutions with desirable, deliberate impact. This validated whether externalities—scenarios that impact communities which never asked to be involved (Burchell 2021)—existed. The solution we'll hand off has already addressed what risks may require mitigation.

In that sprint spirit, now think of each finalist we tested as a prototype. A prototype is a tangible representation or model used to test the potential impact of an idea or design. Think of a prototype as a "dummy" solution that mirrors back how the actual solution will work upon implementation. Through prototypes, we validate what makes the solution both deliberate and desirable. We also look for new pinch points to emerge.

Prototypes come in many formats, some more complex than others. We'll deliver our solutions as low-fidelity prototypes. Low-fidelity (lo-fi) prototypes convey our solutions as "testable artifacts" (Esposito 2018). Through lo-fi, we test the solution for what will resonate with what we know from our proto personas. We can predict improvements without committing the Client to major time and budget investments. While not ready for market, lo-fi prototypes validate future go-to-market strategic planning (Trudeau 2022).

To deliver lo-fi prototypes, we'll practice rapid prototyping. Rapid prototyping fits right into a sprint's need for speed. It involves *quickly* testing a solution, collecting data (such as TBD Observations and/or Interviews), and making changes before delivery. Look for rapid prototyping to feel like lots of quick pinches of reflective thinking.

In-Sights to Be Delivered

Let's reflect back—and deliver forward!—through these constraints about the solution(s) that passed Testing by Defense:

1. Design a lo-fi prototype for each remaining solution to be delivered.
   - ☐ You may only have one solution to deliver. Iterate as needed if other solutions "passed" Testing by Defense.
   - ☐ The prototypes will be delivered as the outcome of your problem-solving actions and all Experiences.
   - ☐ Two prototype techniques are described. Experiment with both as time permits.
   - ☐ Move quickly. Sprint with the spirit of rapid prototyping. Set the whiteboard timer as preferred.
2. Prototype 1: Draw the Solution
   - ☐ Drawings, sketches, and illustrations operate as lo-fi techniques. Each validates your reflective thinking as visualizations. 2D visualizations also inspire others to think about the proposed solution in different ways.
     - ☐ Reflect back: How did you use the whiteboard during each chapter?
     - ☐ Take in all Frames in the whole workspace, like a Disco Ball Mirror. In retrospect, you've framed, mirrored, and delivered lo-fi prototypes in each chapter. You already are a prototype pro!
   - ☐ Create lo-fi drawings to communicate the bare minimum features that differentiate this solution. Think disco ball, not masterpiece.
   - ☐ Use whiteboard features to outline shapes, connect concepts, and upload images. These actions turn abstract ideas into concrete output ready to be delivered as lo-fi prototypes.

3. Prototype 2: A Bisociation Remix
   - ☐ Arthur Koestler's Theory of Bisociation (Popova 2013) inspires this action. While bisociation may be an unfamiliar concept, its presence permeates consumer culture.
     - ☐ *Hangry*, a remix of hungry and angry, appears in the *Oxford English Dictionary*.
     - ☐ *Shrinkflation*, a remix of shrinkage and inflation, trends during periods of economic turmoil.
     - ☐ *Supremium*, a remix of supreme and premium, injects a new level of status in sectors ranging from energy to entertainment.
     - ☐ *Mastige*, a remix of mass and prestige, describes higher pricing on products with wide distribution.
       - ☐ The list goes on: ecopreneurship, edutainment, frenemy, brunch, dotmocracy (see page xxxix), and many more.
     - ☐ Brand collaborations also offer evidence of widespread bisociation. When unaffiliated brands co-design product lines, they remix their best, often unrelated, qualities. The result signals their attempt at transformative, better, and desirable solutions not yet seen by consumers.
   - ☐ How might we remix the analogous features from two solutions into one prototype?
     - ☐ View your finalists as analogous to each other. From Chapter 1, we know that analogous describes "feels like" similarities.
     - ☐ Reflect back: Which features from the two solutions might be combined?
     - ☐ Look for features that enhance Touch Points, create easier actions, and redirect Turning Points.
     - ☐ What would be achieved by delivering the features as a remixed solution? What benefits materialize from a combination? How would the combination leverage the opportunity defined by the colorful space?
     - ☐ If you already attempted Prototype 1, what made that drawing difficult? How might a bisociated prototype work around that difficulty and effectively express desirable, deliberate impact?

- ☐ Merge the selected features by drawing the remixed prototype.
- ☐ Stay open to iterate, trying combinations and rearrangements while maintaining a rapid pace.
- ☐ If you start to feel like you are creating a Frankensteined solution, keep going!
- ☐ Trying to remix more than two solutions can produce the effects of a collage. The Empathy Mirror included collaging. In retrospect, that Experience primed us to prototype this reflection.
- ☐ Merge images of the aspirational features to show the solution's essence. This helps others see your thinking when the features do not yet precisely exist.
  - ☐ Search press releases, trend reports, and libraries of free, licensed digital images for additional inspiration.
  - ☐ Look for brand collaborations or popular culture references. Extract their qualities to validate your prototype.

Another lo-fi option is a paper prototype. Just as you do not need to be an engineer to model in 3D, you do not need to be an artist to draw. Paper prototypes provide a change of scenery. They bring your whiteboard work off a URL screen and onto an IRL sheet of paper. Imagine the offline equivalent of each whiteboard tool, and you have your supply list. You can also easily take a picture of your drawing(s) and upload it to the whiteboard.

Your practice with sticky notes to convey written ideas pays off here too. What will you build in 3D form with a pile of 3″ × 3″ sticky notes? Square by square, you deliver your version of the lo-fi disco ball.

End With a Start in Mind(set)

From deleting and editing to testing and prototyping, we moved through the second problem-solving diamond. By inserting uncertain moments ahead of delivery, we actively tested our optimism. This test did not have a "right" or a "wrong" answer. By defending optimistic solutions, we protected the Client from future, risky uncertainty. That's something to celebrate.

We've arrived at the very finish line that uncertainty initially obstructed. But, maybe some foggy uncertainty remains on our Disco Ball Mirror. If you used your finger to draw emojis on that foggy surface, how would you represent your Whole Human Mindset? Even with ongoing uncertainty, how pinched are your hands, heart, and head at this final point?

Find space in or around the Chapter 4 Frame. Take three minutes to draw or upload three emojis that describe the pinches you're experiencing. What does the pinch alert you to? What does it make your hands notice? Your heart? Your head?

Now, consider how you can reframe those pinches to point you to deliver optimism for implementation. How will you cast your reflections back into action for future Challenges?

To Be Deleted! in Business Research

Apply To Be Deleted! as a starting point for data analysis planning or data preparation. Planning for analysis includes efforts to validate, edit, code, and count data.

☐ Before planning begins, reflect on all product solutions generated during To Be Deleted!. What patterns emerge that link solutions to qualitative data, including observation and interview data?

☐ Qualitative data analysis requires data reduction, categorization, and coding. Use To Be Deleted! as a code sheet to support these activities.

    ☐ Each solution becomes a code or a link between the possible solution and the data set. Codes verify if solutions appear in the data in meaningful ways.

    ☐ Look for verbatims in interview transcripts. Which quotes resonate with solutions identified as goods, services, experiences, or ideas?

    ☐ Use the code sheet to support, contradict, or expand observational data.

□ Similarly, use To Be Deleted! as a code sheet for any open-ended questions included in quantitative, descriptive surveys.

Use To Be Deleted! as a thought starter to code solutions with constraints in mind.

□ Data analysis planning increases researchers' familiarity with their data sets. It also reveals response rates, missing data, and threats to validity before analysis.

□ Use the "sweet spot of innovation" (see page 13) constraints to supplement the code sheet. As patterns emerge among codes, "eyeball" the data to detect whether the patterns also represent:

  □ Desirability, or what people actually want

  □ Feasibility, or the technical requirements to deliver what people want

  □ Viability, a business model equipped for peoples' needs and technical requirements

Testing by Defense in Business Research

Apply Testing by Defense as a preliminary exercise to identify limitations.

Communicating limitations can be confused with delivering "bad news" to decision-makers. It takes practice to communicate limitations while inspiring actions. Ultimately, this results in trust and transparency.

- ☐ Before listing limitations in a final research report, reflect on consequences revealed during Testing by Defense.
  - ☐ How do these consequences introduce limitations, thus challenging trustworthy recommendations?
- ☐ Look for sources of error, weak or exaggerated logic, overstated generalizability, and other threats to accuracy and credibility. Limitations like these likely appear in Not Desirable × Not Deliberate intersection.
  - ☐ Compare these limitations to all Testing by Defense consequences.
  - ☐ To maintain decision-makers' confidence, communicate the comparison with transparency.

Use Testing by Defense as a thought starter to strengthen recommendations.

A final research report provides recommendations. Recommendations transform data-driven solutions into actions that resolve research objectives. They offer differentiated, inimitable value to the business.

- ☐ Limitations are to the research process as constraints are to the design thinking process. When effectively communicated, both strengthen recommendations as iterative, actionable outcomes.
  - ☐ Limitations outline opportunities to improve future decisions related to the research process.
  - ☐ Constraints point to opportunities to frame related research questions for future endeavors.

To evaluate recommendations for transparency, use the sweeter spot reframe (see page 20). Look for recommendations to represent outcomes that are:

- ☐ Transformative, based on Truths for humanity and planet.
- ☐ Better, based on built-in Beliefs of purpose-driven businesses.
- ☐ Desirable, based on Decisions that serve whole people's authentic needs.

Closing Retrospective

To Be Determined!

Reflect on a Challenge that required your determination. Hold up a mirror to that moment. What would reflect back? If you were to draw that Challenge on a whiteboard, what would it look like? What surrounded you? What were you doing? How did your determination change what you were doing? What would you compare your determination to? How did you celebrate your determination?

Four Frames, eight Experiences. Whiteboard workspaces filled with pain points, pulse points, and pinch points. We diverged to generate out-sights and discerned to synthesize in-sights. We reflected to validate our evolving tbds. We first sought a colorful problem and then solved for colorful spaces. From vulnerable Beginner's Mirrors to optimistic Disco Ball Mirrors, our hands, hearts, and heads de-drabbed business as usual.

As we acted and reflected with the uncertainty of TBD, we deepened another posture. In retrospect, a fifth posture pointed to this conclusion from our start. We started at the end without even knowing it. As Milton Glaser once said, "We're always looking, but we never really see" (Barnes).

To close this Challenge, reframe how you verbalize TBD's inflection. Say "to be determined" out loud at least two times, changing how you emphasize each word. Notice what you hear. Does an analogous expression join the usual sound of uncertainty? Our familiar adage may sound less like the downtick of a weary question mark. The dot, dot, dot of a shrugged decrescendo disappeared. We may now also detect the uptick of a *determined* exclamation point. A crescendo of more certainty. Temporarily not knowing merged with enthusiasm for personal drive. As our tbds expanded, the usual meaning of TBD (described in the Introduction) also expanded. We gradually offset our hesitancy to act with the determination to keep going. We were unsure at first, but then became determined as we saw things differently. We acted on the difference between thinking "We don't get where we are going" and "We get to create where we are going."

Determination, like each chapter's posture, plays a valuable role in workplaces. According to Freier (2021), workplaces that foster determination benefit the whole organization. Challenges arise quickly at work, like a never-ending game of funhouse whack-a-mole. When organizations do not value determination, employees brace for stagnation. Organizations need to inspire us to seek and solve colorful problems, to co-design and collaborate, and think in new ways. With determination, none of this needs *to be daunting*.

Uniting EL and DT *checked the diamonds* on how to discover, define, develop, and deliver determination in workplaces. Everything we experienced represented a workaround, shortcut, or reframe of tricky concepts with sticky workplace implications. For example, observations, white spaces, and retrospectives generate their fair share of resistance. Each concept has multiple interpretations, exposing people's tbds to judgment. Expect the pain points from those mistaken "soft skills" to be constant, even with iteration and practice. When you think by design, however, you act and reflect with two types of determination on your side.

The subtle reframe of determined represents more than convenient wordsmithing. Like lo-fi prototypes, remixing what seems bare minimum validates why we need to seek and solve. Transformative, better, desirable solutions do not require overhauling entire contexts. Some celebrated transformations, in fact, remix only 3%. According to designer and entrepreneur Virgil Abloh, "[a] 3% [change] expands our worldview, without pushing our zones of comfort to the brink. We're exposed to 'new,' but not eccentric or disconcerting" (Abloh 2021; Phan 2023). Articulating "determined" in two ways might be so subtle it borders on drab. Yet, bare minimums hold power to open whole new discussions.

Abloh's 3% Rule models how we can package and carry our personal determination into future Challenges. His 3% "cheat code" originates in *Personal Design Language*, Abloh's "seven-point manifesto" (Silbert 2017) that outlines his truths, beliefs, and defenses about colorful problems. A manifesto is "a statement of purpose and a script for action" (Burgess 2022). Brands increasingly use manifestos instead of "dull mission statements" (Getman 2018) as differentiators. Consumer activists interested in

ESG (environmental, social, governance) initiatives continue to scrutinize the sincerity of mission statements. As consumers make more decisions motivated by CSR, brands promote manifestos to reassert their authentic cultures as more than boilerplate language. Lifestyle brands Lululemon and Patagonia trailblazed the use of manifestos to change how people think about well-being and sustainability. Moleskine, Warby Parker, Levi's, Nespresso, and Kia also use manifestos to share action-oriented stories that integrate with their core messages. Brands with manifestos activate more than their mission, vision, and values. A manifesto takes a stance and supports how a brand *postures*. Consumers, eager to form meaningful relationships with brands, want to see their identities reflected in the bold conversations that manifestos stimulate.

The 3% Rule, and manifestos in general, offer all whole humans an actionable tool. Manifestos codify our personal postures and inspire action and reflection when we face colorful problems. They share stories about how our tbds navigate and celebrate uncertainty. People connect with Abloh and other brands' manifestos because they are relatable and slightly experimental. They replace the intimidation of uncertainty with an arc of unmistakable determination.

How might we create our own manifestos that mirror the double meaning of to be determined? Let's use another acronym as a lens for this final HMW. To create your own manifesto, apply MAYA: Most Advanced Yet Acceptable (Friis, 2021). MAYA puts three constraints on how to design individual manifestos. First, MAYA reminds us that what's familiar can also be novel. Familiar novelty goes hand-in-hand with simplicity. Simplicity requires restraint, a tight edit of only necessities, not nice-to-haves. Finally, MAYA reassures us that experiences over time advance our thinking. Unsprints will incrementally add up to sprints.

When Challenges test your tbds, a MAYA manifesto redirects how you accept complex, colorful problems. You want to experience uncertainty's upside, the desirable outcomes made possible by unexpected experiences. At the same time, you don't want to be discouraged by uncomfortable uncertainty. That combination makes it difficult for you to make a desirable impact.

You can count on workplace Challenges to always involve co-design with clients, community, and whole humans. While the context of every

Challenge varies, a MAYA manifesto follows you, like portable protection for future pain, pulse, and pinch points.

As metaphors inspire us to think in images, manifestos inspire us to think in stories. To design your manifesto, mirror your own version of MAYA's three constraints.

Act and Reflect: Make Your Manifesto Mirror

You can make a Manifesto Mirror in three steps. Each step integrates the principles of MAYA. What you make may at first resemble a lower fidelity prototype than you prefer. Trust your tbds. The pain points of the first iteration will become the pulse points of later Challenges. As you act and reflect on those Challenges, determine the pinch points that make your Manifesto Mirror whole. Each iteration reveals your personal tbds and adds color to your unique approach to think by design.

- ☐ Think about thinking.

    During the Challenge, we integrated four Retrospectives as our moments for reflective thinking. Use those Retrospectives to now inspire metacognition, or "a way of thinking about one's thinking in order to grow" (Cultivating Reflection and Metacognition, n.d.). Reflect on each retrospective to distinguish uniquely positive moments that stood out to you. Remind yourself about the pinch points that colored the Challenge. What were the moments that now appear *to be desirable*? The ones that reflect the upside of uncertainty? What trends do you notice across all four Retrospectives? Does anything go against the trend?

- ☐ Mirror others' manifestos.

    Look to brand examples of manifestos as inspiration. What do you notice about how local brands or small businesses use manifestos? How do their manifestos differentiate their postures from their mission and values? How do these compare with national or global brand manifestos?

- ☐ Frame your format.

    As you built Frames to document your Experiences and Retrospectives, you now need a Frame to format your Manifesto Mirror.

Which idea(s) from this list excite you? Per page 100, bisociate as you prefer!

- Infographics: Visualize a data-driven story that incorporates or inspires your tbds.
    - Use reflections on your TBD Observations and Interviews as data. How did other environments and other people support your experiences? What can you narrate as a beginning, middle, and to-be-determined ending?
- Dear uncertainty letters: Write a letter that genuinely expresses how you approach Challenges.
    - If a "love letter" to uncertainty seems like too much, first try to write a "break-up letter" (Singletary 2023). Explain what would make you abandon your appreciation of cloud problems to revert to clock problems.
    - If the length of a letter seems overwhelming, frame a postcard. Pair a short and sweet message with a compelling "wish you [uncertainty] were here" image.
- Future press releases: Popularized by Amazon (Gallo 2019), a future press release elicits your radical acceptance that uncertainty does not go away. You commit to an uncertain road ahead but with an eye for kaleidoscopic complexities. By starting with an end in mind (as you've backcasted to close each chapter), you assert how you will determinedly act and reflect.
    - Title your manifesto and list a new Challenge.
    - Talk about why your approach is colorful and determined.
    - Describe how you'll start your actions and integrate your reflections.
    - Brag about what differentiates your approach.
- Customize an acronym: What combination of letters might reflect your personal rally cry when Challenges emerge? *TBD* is itself a manifesto. Its meaning provides peace of mind that not knowing is desirable. Don't sweat it if the acronym you build does not already hold established meaning like *TBD*.

If the series of letters captures meaning for you, that's what matters.

☐ Create a fill-in-the-blank one-liner: This format resembles POVs. Distill a couple of tbds you see as applicable to *many* Challenges. Iterate a few versions of the one-liner. This format's goal is to identify a fill-in-the-blank that flexes with Challenges and maintains your tbds.

Postface

To demonstrate Manifesto Mirrors, I invited a few celebrated practitioners to reflect on what makes them determined. What you'll read bisociates fill-in-the-blank one-liners that also mirror *Think by Design's* acronym. I'm grateful for what each Manifesto Mirror reflects and deeply admire the whole human behind each mirror as an inspiring co-designer.* Celebrate their determination as a colorful start to cast your reflections back into action.

☐ When I remix Experiential Learning with Design Thinking, I see how **to be daring**.
  ☐ Patrick Green, Executive Director, Center for Engaged Learning, Teaching, and Scholarship, Loyola University Chicago
☐ Practicing Design Thinking within Experiential Learning means I get **to be drastically wrong!**
  ☐ Alley Neary, J.D. Candidate, George Washington University Law School
☐ Practicing Design Thinking within Business Education means I get **to be divergent**.
  ☐ Brenden Oeth, Solutions Engineer, Salesforce
☐ Practicing Design Thinking within Business Education means I get **to be deviceful**.
  ☐ Maria Marcus, Digital Marketing Coach, BxB Media

---

* For more backstory about these Mirror Manifestos, see Appendix 2.

- Celebrating Business Education and Design Thinking means I get **to be dynamic.**
  - Vaishnavi Vembar, Marketing, CrowdDoing
- Practicing Design Thinking within Business Education means I get **to be dexterous**.
  - Ben Wiedmaier, Senior Content Marketing Manager, User Interviews; Adjunct Professor, DePaul University
- Celebrating Business Education and Design Thinking means I get **to be distinctive.**
  - Chris Robinson, Product Design Lead, McKinsey & Company
- Celebrating Business Education and Design Thinking means I get **to be decisive.**
  - Maureen Baynes, Senior Experience Design Consultant, Slalom
- Celebrating Business Education and Design Thinking means I get **to be diligent, decomposing, and depositing.**
  - Kelsey Doolittle, Research, Customer Strategy, UX Design Consultant, Slalom
- Celebrating Business Education and Design Thinking means I get **to be direct** in my insights.
  - Diana Kelter, Associate Director of North America Trends, Mintel
- Celebrating Business Education and Design Thinking means I get **to be dancing** on the cutting edge of progressive and sustainable business strategy development.
  - Nic Dimond, Design and Innovation Leader, Salesforce Design
- Celebrating Business Education and Design Thinking means I get **to be daydreaming** about a more equitable, sustainable, and prosperous future.
  - Lauren Peters Lague, CMO, Black Girls Code; Chair, Board of Directors, Catapult Design

- ☐ Practicing Design Thinking within Business Education means I get **to be deliberate**.
  - ☐ Denise Burchell, Design and Innovation Leader, Salesforce Design
- ☐ When I remix Business Education with Design Thinking, I see how **to be duo!**
  - ☐ Rafael Robles, Co-Founder, Duo Development
- ☐ Celebrating Business Education and Design Thinking means I get **to be dependable**.
  - ☐ Tulsi Patel, Analyst, Grainger

Appendixes

Appendix 1

Brief of the Colorful Problem

From:	**To:**
Description of a current Challenge. A Challenge reflects a real-world scenario that needs a real-world solution. It centers on whole humans who face a colorful problem.	Description of a future, imagined solution. What reflects the most colorful solution? One that pushes against the diamond edges?
Success:	**Why:**
Description of what a hand-off at delivery looks & feels like. What does 'done' mean? Does it reflect: Facts & figures? Story & philosophy? A blend of both?	Description of what's at stake for whole humans. What makes this whole Challenge resonate, hands, heart, and head? What reflects a more colorful experience?

Figure A.1 Challenge Brief template

Appendix 2: Mirror Manifesto Backstories

The first word that came to my mind is daring—risk-taking, change-oriented, fresh, new, orientated toward creativity and imagination, centered on hope. I think the change that needs to happen in education is really an exercise in creativity and imagination—which requires one to be daring, to mix foundational ideas (theories) with practice and lessons learned from practice, remixing them to garner new ideas, theories, and practices. I wish I had stumbled into design thinking sooner as it provides a pathway, a framework, and reflective pattern to accompany experiential learning. The scaffolding that design thinking provides helps center the learning and reflection in fresh relevant ways, while honoring the experience of the individual. Design thinking is like a series of moons (reflections) that revolve around a planet (experience-based learning), offering multiple perspectives and new learning.

—Patrick Green

While at first glance this may sound negative, being "drastically wrong" has been at the center of my design thinking and experiential learning journey. The crux of design thinking is the pivot from an original idea to a more client centered approach. Being wrong isn't the mistake, rather resistance to change and experimentation is what prohibits truly effective marketing. Sometimes the genius is within the last sketch, client meeting, or research insight instead of the firsts of client-based marketing.

—Alley Neary

When practicing Design Thinking, no idea or answer is "bad" or "wrong." Design Thinking embraces (and welcomes!) ambiguity— it's baked into the process of empathizing, iterating, prototyping, testing, and ultimately implementing. However, when we think of a classroom setting, the binary of "right" and "wrong" is often associated. Exams have correct answers. Students either pass or fail. So on and so forth. Moreover, business education is meant to prepare students for the "real" world, and with that is the reality that many things in a business setting shift and change from their original starting point. The world of business is, at its core, always divergent, whether by design, or human intervention. Therefore, it's quintessential that business education takes this into account when preparing the next generation of students to enter the workforce. By practicing Design Thinking within Business Education, you're breaking down the binary of "right" and "wrong" that's embedded in student's brains and instead, encouraging them to solve business challenges with an iterative, divergent process

—Brenden Oeth

Design Thinking brings incentive creative thinking to traditional Business Education and has prepared me to be ready for all sorts of real-world situations.

—Maria Marcus

There is never one right answer when joining the two concepts together. I believe it is encouraged to think differently, as the way we look at

Business evolves by the second. What matters is how you expose yourself to trying new things, how to research for a project and client, or how you conduct research overall.

—Vaishnavi Vembar

The best businesses, regardless of focus, balance innovation with structure, leveraging design thinking, agile workflows, and use sound fundamentals to offer a space to play.

—Ben Wiedmaier

Figuring out how to be distinctive in my career took time and many setbacks. Being distinctive required learning from my setbacks and trying over and over again. More importantly, it required a constant belief in myself, my ideas and what I bring to the table. For me, that is design thinking in a nutshell.

—Chris Robinson

I can help organizations be more confident in the direction they are taking by validating hypotheses and possible solutions with user research and input from real customers. Building more human-centered businesses allows us to solve real problems, together.

—Maureen Baynes

For me, everything I do in my life comes down to connection. And design thinking helps me be people-first and designing for the end-users in an empathetic way. Solving problems is hard unless you break it down into small chunks, and design thinking is a helpful structure to break down the BIG chunks of problems into manageable steps. If we want to make the world a better place, a good way to do it is within the structure of the society in which we live. It validates our truths, because living your values truly matters when something is on the line in terms of sacrifice, when you have something to LOSE. And within the business context, you have lots to lose. So it's a powerful way to put your beliefs to the test. I think design thinking is an effective LIFE tool. Establishing a clear problem statement, doing research into the problem, and developing potential solutions: hello to making life

easier. But within business context, it is a structure that kickstarts the potential to solve REAL WORLD big issues. And being able to do that is AWESOME. I think for me, the timing on learning this was fine, but now that I've got the knowledge, I'm only going up, not going back
—Kelsey Doolittle

An idea without a plan will always stay a dream and merging the worlds of business and design allows my creativity and logic to flourish.
—Diana Kelter

It's cool to have language that is persuasive to business and also inspires us to keep humans at the center of the solutions we're imaging and building.

—Nic Dimond

Practicing Design Thinking within Business Education means I get to be dabblin' in new tools and processes that will ultimately produce more successful outcomes.
  When I remix Business Education with Design Thinking, I see how to be damning of decades-old dogmas (biases) and their diminishing returns and free to create remarkable innovation that meets the needs of interdependent stakeholders. ;)
—Lauren Peters Lague

When we put design thinking and business together, we get to design for disproportionate impact. That's because business is the single biggest lever for change in our society, and design thinking helps us create that change for people and with them. We create new products, services, and experiences that resonate, solve problems, change minds and behaviors, and connect people.

—Denise Burchell

The world is a complicated place, and designed interventions can't come from (or be implemented by) one field or practice group alone. At Duo, everything is a "remix"! We call our practice "Multicontextual Design" because we recognize the world to be composed of a variety of contexts (subjects, environments, objects, and influencing factors) that are nested and interacting. When creating anything new for the world, we bring in elements from a variety of contexts to create a more positive reality for people and their environment.

Business strategy falls in what we call "norm-making" because the tools of those trades are meant to influence the way people behave, what they purchase, the objects they use, etc. But Design Thinking falls in what we call "form-making" because the tools of design give physical form to ideas. Traditionally business would come up with an idea and then ask designers to bring it to life. We practice what we call "Norm/Form-Making" which simultaneously "remixes" these practices and methodologies to give form to new norms that will bring a positive outcome to society.

This is the power of the combination of these practices - changing our mindset from "what problems are we solving?" to "what realities are we creating?" so that we can create more ethical realities for all people and our shared environment.

—Rafael Robles

When addressing complex challenges, it is crucial to set forth a comprehensive approach. As business-minded people we tend to focus on conventional solutions that are driven by feasible and viable outcomes. However, it is crucial to resolve problems with a design thinking approach because it enables us to create solutions that promote desirable results. The combination of business education and design thinking is powerful because it allows us to lean into strategic thinking through a user-centric lens. By emphasizing with the end-user(s), we can be deliberate in providing relevant and impactful solutions to meet real needs. A balanced approach taught me to be dynamic to ever-changing conditions to ensure I make informed and innovative decisions catered to the end-user(s). Ultimately, a holistic approach has prepared me to deliver well-rounded, thoughtful, and realistic solutions tailored to unique needs and challenges so that I can be a dependable partner.

—Tulsi Patel

References

"5 Whys Template Example." n.d. Miro. https://miro.com/templates/5-whys/, (accessed September 15, 2023).

"The Other Side of Empathy." July 31, 2017. dschool. https://dschool.stanford .edu/news-events/the-other-side-of-empathy#:~:text=Essentially%2C%20 if%20you're%20not,could%20be%20verbal%20or%20mental.

Abloh, V. 2021. "The Percentage of Creativity is 3%, According to Virgil Abloh." *DOMUS*. www.domusweb.it/en/design/2021/09/21/the-percentage-of-creativity .html.

Ackerman, R. 2023. "Design Thinking Was Supposed to Fix the World. Where Did It Go Wrong?" *MIT Technology Review*. www.technologyreview.com /2023/02/09/1067821/design-thinking-retrospective-what-went-wrong/.

Adams, G., B.A. Converse, A. Hales, and L. Klotz. February 2022. "When Subtraction Adds Value." *Harvard Business Review*. https://hbr.org/2022/02 /when-subtraction-adds-value.

Alita, J. 2021. "Principle of Closure in Visual Design." Nielsen Norman Group. www.nngroup.com/articles/principle-closure/.

Anderson-Stanier, N. 2022. "How Might We Statements: A Powerful Way to Turn Insights Into Opportunities." dscout. https://dscout.com/people-nerds /how-might-we-statements.

Anderson-Stanier, N. n.d. "When It's Worth Conducting Research With Non-Users." dscout. https://dscout.com/people-nerds/research-non-users.

Asana. 2022. "19 Unconscious Bias Examples and How to Prevent Them." Asana. https://asana.com/resources/unconscious-bias-examples.

Barnes, S. 2020. "20 Memorable Quotes by the Late Milton Glaser to Inspire the Designer in You." My Modern Met. https://mymodernmet.com/milton-glaser-quotes/.

Battarbee, K., J. Fulton, and S.G. Howard. n.d. *Empathy on the Edge*. https:// newideocom.s3.amazonaws.com/assets/files/pdfs/news/Empathy_on_the_ Edge.pdf.

Bell, A. 2023. "How the Global Rise in Anxiety Can Be a Catalyst for Change." WGSN. www.wgsn.com/en/blogs/how-global-rise-anxiety-can-be-catalyst-change.

Beer, J. 2016. *Patagonia's Business Manifesto Still Ahead of Its Time 10 Years Later*. Fast Company. www.fastcompany.com/3063438/patagonias-business-manifesto-still-ahead-of-its time-ten-years-later.

Beran, S.N. 2022. "Gen Z in the Classroom: A Guide to Applying Experiential Learning to Design and UX." Dscout. https://dscout.com/people-nerds/gen-z-classroom-guide.

Bergmann, B. and J. Bergmann. 2021. *Mau.*

Blijlevens, J. 2021. "Educating Marketing Students to Understand Designers' Thought-Worlds." *Journal of Marketing Education* 45, no. 1, pp. 1837.

Blum, S.D., ed. 2020. *Ungrading: Why Rating Students Undermines Learning (and What to Do Instead)*. West Virginia University Press.

Brown, A.M. 2021. "Experience Design: 4 Ways to Make Your Next Event Unforgettable." IDEO U. www.ideou.com/blogs/inspiration/experience-design-4-ways-to-make-your-next-event-unforgettable.

Buchanan, R. 1992. "Wicked Problems in Design Thinking." *Design Issues* 8, no. 2, pp. 521.

Burchell, D. 2022. "Create Effective How Might We Statements." Trailhead. https://trailhead.salesforce.com/content/learn/modules/challenge-framing-and-scoping/create-effective-how-might-we-statements.

Burchell, D. 2021. "Designers Need to Move People and Pixels | by Denise Burchell Salesforce Designer." Medium. https://medium.com/salesforce-ux/designers-need-to-move-people-and-pixels-3e6759ecccbf.

Burgess-Auburn, C. 2022. *You Need a Manifesto*. Stanford d.school. https://dschool.stanford.edu/book-collections/you-need-a-manifesto.

Canvs Editorial. 2021. "Context in Design: A Keystone to Understanding Users." Medium. https://uxdesign.cc/context-in-design-a-keystone-to-understanding-users-aeba93ce5dc4.

Caeiro Rodriguez, M. and M.J. Fernández Iglesias. 2019. "He Point of View in Design Thinking." ResearchGate. www.researchgate.net/publication/348097976_The_Point_of_View_in_Design_Thinking.

Carter, C. and Stanford d.school. 2022. *The Secret Language of Maps: How to Tell Visual Stories with Data*. N.p.: Clarkson Potter/Ten Speed.

Castrillon, C. 2021. "How to Cultivate Empathy in the Workplace." Forbes. www.forbes.com/sites/carolinecastrillon/2021/08/15/how-to-cultivate-empathy-in-the-workplace.

Chayka, K. 2021. "We All Have 'Main-Character Energy' Now." The New Yorker. www.newyorker.com/culture/infinite-scroll/we-all-have-main-character-energynow.

Chi, C. 2023. "How to Craft a Brand Manifesto." HubSpot Blog https://blog.hubspot.com/marketing/brand-manifesto#what-is-a-bm.

"Constraints in design." n.d. Figma. www.figma.com/resource-library/constraints-indesign/.

Crockow, E.M. 2018. "How Many Decisions Do We Make Each Day?" Psychology

Today. www.psychologytoday.com/us/blog/stretching-theory/201809/how-many-decisions-do-we-make-each-day.

"Cultivating Reflection and Metacognition." n.d. College of LSA. https://lsa.umich .edu/content/dam/sweetland-assets/sweetland-documents/teaching resources/CultivatingReflectionandMetacognition/Metacognition.pdf.

Deeb, G. 2022. "Don't Apply a "One-Size-Fits-All" Approach to Your Marketing. Do This Instead." Entrepreneur. www.entrepreneur.com/growing-a-business /dont-apply-aone-size-fits-all-approach-to-your/427996.

Eisermann, R. n.d. "The Double Diamond Design Process—Still Fit for Purpose?" Medium. https://medium.com/design-council/the-double-diamond-design-process-still-fit-for-purpose-fc619bbd2ad3.

Emmer, M. 2018. "95 Percent of New Products Fail. Here Are 6 Steps to Make Sure Yours Don't." Inc. www.inc.com/marc-emmer/95-percent-of-new-products-fail-here-are-6-steps-to-make-sure-yours-dont.html.

Episode 230: Salesforce CFO Emeritus Mark Hawkins's Career is "Better, Better, Never Done." 2021. ICE. www.ice.com/insights/conversations/inside-the-ice-house/salesforce-cfo-emeritus-mark-hawkins-career-is-better-better-never-done.

Esposito, E. 2018. "Low-Fidelity vs. High-Fidelity Prototyping." InVision. www .invisionapp.com/inside-design/low-fi-vs-hi-fi-prototyping/.

Faith, K. 2019. "Design Thinking's Missing Piece." Medium. https://karenfaith .medium.com/design-thinkings-missing-piece-99062069403f.

Fink, L.D. 1999. "A Model of Active Learning." https://commons.trincoll.edu /ctl/files/2013/08/Week-3-Active-Learning.pdf.

Finzi, B., M. Lipton, and V. Firth. 2019. "A Beginner's Mindset." Deloitte. www2.deloitte.com/content/dam/insights/us/articles/4814_A-beginners-mindset/4814%20A%20Beginner%27s%20mindset.pdf.

Fealy, L., dir. 2022. *The World's To Do List: We Need Urgent Action | The Global Goals*. www.youtube.com/watch?v=uWtIZJ3EhGY.

Friis, R. 2021. "The MAYA Principle: Design for the Future, but Balance it With Your Users' Present." The Interaction Design Foundation. www.interaction-design.org/literature/article/design-for-the-future-but-balance-it-with-your-users-present.

Friis, R. and T. Yu. 2023. "5 Common Low-Fidelity Prototypes and Their Best Practices." Interaction Design Foundation. www.interaction-design.org/literature /article/prototyping-learn-eight-common-methods-and-best-practices%20.

Freier, L. December 15, 2021. "How Self-Determination Can Boost Satisfaction at Work." Physcology Today. www.psychologytoday.com/us/blog/anxiety-attack/202112/how-self-determination-can-boost-satisfaction-work.

Gallo, C. 2019. "Jeff Bezos Requires Amazon's Leaders to Perform This Powerful

Ritual Before Launching Anything." Inc. www.inc.com/carmine-gallo/jeff-bezos-requires-amazons-leaders-to-perform-this-powerful-ritual-before-launching-anything.html.

Gambini, B. 2017. *Study Shows 'Walking a Mile in Their Shoes' May Be Hazardous to Your Health.* University at Buffalo. www.buffalo.edu/news/releases/2017/05/016.html.

Getman, C. 2018. "17 Inspiring Brand Manifestos." The Agency Arsenal. https://theagencyarsenal.com/12-inspiring-brand-manifestos/.

Gibbons, S. 2018. "Using Prioritization Matrices to Inform UX Decisions." Nielsen Norman Group. www.nngroup.com/articles/prioritization-matrices/.

Gino, Francesca. September–October 2018. "The Business Case for Curiosity." *Harvard Business Review.* https://hbr.org/2018/09/the-business-case-for-curiosity.

Grefe, R. 2012. "Head, Heart and Hand: Modern Design Practice." AIGA San Antonio. https://sanantonio.aiga.org/head-heart-and-hand-modern-design-practice/.

Haden, J. 2023. "Emotionally Intelligent Leaders Use the 3 Percent Rule to Bypass Hesitation and Fear, and Help People Embrace New Ideas, Products, and Processes." Inc. www.inc.com/jeff-haden/emotionally-intelligent-leaders-use-the3-percent-rule-to-bypass-hesitation-fear-help-people-embrace-new-ideas-products-processes.html.

Hambeukers, D. 2020. "Design Is More Than Problem Solving." Medium. https://medium.com/design-leadership-notebook/design-is-more-than-problem-solving-7e290535927c.

Hasan, S. 2023. "When Did 'Wholesome' Become a Gen Z Compliment?" The New York Times. www.nytimes.com/2023/05/11/style/gen-z-wholesome.html.

Hilton Segel, L. and H. Hatami. 2022. *Mind the Gap: Curated Reads for Gen Z—and their Z-Curious Colleagues.* McKinsey & Company. www.mckinsey.com/~/media/mckinsey/email/genz/2022/12/20/2022-12-20aa.html.

Houston, A. 2023. ""Sneakerheads" Are Driving Growth of Athletic Footwear Market: YouGov Report." Retail Dive. www.retaildive.com/press-release/20230321-sneakerheads-are-driving-growth-of-athletic-footwear-market-yougov-repor/.

"How to Hit the Innovation Sweet Spot and Why It's Not All That Straightforward." n.d. Board of Innovation. www.boardofinnovation.com/blog/how-to-hit-the-innovation-sweet-spot/.

"How to Use Sprints to Work Smart and Upskill." 2022. IDEO U. www.ideou.com/blogs/inspiration/how-to-use-sprints-to-work-smart-and-upskill.

IDEO. n.d. "Design Thinking Frequently Asked Questions." IDEO Design

Thinking. https://designthinking.ideo.com/faq/how-do-people-define-design-thinking.

Jacobs, A.J. 2016. "UX: Creating Proto-Personas." UX Collective. https://uxdesign.cc/ux-creating-proto-personas-76a1738401a2.

Katz, R. 2020. "How To Run a Consequence Scanning Workshop." Medium. https://medium.com/salesforce-ux/how-to-run-a-consequence-scanning-workshop-4b14792ea987.

King, P.M. and K.S. Kitchener. 1994. *Developing reflective judgment: understanding and promoting intellectual growth and critical thinking in adolescents and adults.* Hoboken, NJ, New Jersey: Wiley.

Kozyreva, A., S. Wineburg, S. Lewandowsky, and R. Hertwig. September 2022. "Critical Ignoring as a Core Competence for Digital Citizens." *Current Directions in Psychological Science* 32, no. 1, pp. 8188. https://doi.org/10.25740/gk771kw4093.

Kristof, N. September 16, 2023. "Opinion | Coming Soon in New York: Cocktails, Steak and Hypocrisy." The New York Times. www.nytimes.com/2023/09/16/opinion/un-sustainability-goals-poverty.html.

Krippendorff, K. 2022. "3 Things You're Doing Wrong When You Try to Plan for the Future." Fast Company. www.fastcompany.com/90732637/3-things-youre-doing-wrong-when-you-try-to-plan-for-the-future.

Krockow, E. 2018. "How Many Decisions Do We Make Each Day?" Psychology Today. www.psychologytoday.com/us/blog/stretching-theory/201809/how-many-decisions-do-we-make-each-day.

Last, J. 2023. "Power of Optimism Shows Value of Sports Fans." The Marketing Insider. www.mediapost.com/publications/article/382525/power-of-optimism-shows-value-of-sports-fans.html.

"Learn the Enterprise Design Thinking Framework—Enterprise Design Thinking." n.d. IBM. www.ibm.com/design/thinking/page/framework/keys/playbacks.

Maghraby, S. and F. Oswald. 2021. "Design Thinking in a Nutshell." openSAP. https://open.sap.com/courses/dt2.

Mau, B. 2020. *Bruce Mau: MC24: Bruce Mau S 24 Principles for Designing Massive Change in Your Life and Work.* J. Ward, Ed. Phaidon Press.

Merritt, E. 2017. "Walk a Mile in My Shoes: Closing the Empathy Deficit." American Alliance of Museums. www.aam-us.org/2017/05/01/empathy-a-mile-in-my-shoes-closing-the-empathy-deficit/.

Melendez, S. 2023. "Figma's Collaborative Tools Could Change the Way Everyone Works." Fast Company. www.fastcompany.com/90931685/figmas-collaborative-figjam-spotlight?utm_source=newsletters&utm_medium=email&utm_campaign=FC%20-%20Compass%20Newsletter.Newsletter

%20-%20FC%20-%20Compass%209-2-23&leadId=380897&mkt_tok =NjEwLUxFRS04NzIAAAGN9ObMeGI1t3Ai7.

Miklas, R. 2015. "Loyalty and the Opposite of Surprise & Delight." Quality Incentive Company. https://qualityincentivecompany.com/blog/loyalty-and-the-opposite-of-surprise-delight/.

Miller, E. 2020. "Using the Mindsets of Relationship Design to Show Up and Make a Difference in Times of Crisis." Medium. https://medium.com /salesforce-ux/how-the-mindsets-of-relationship-design-are-showing-up-in-a-pandemic-19e58e05197c.

Mollick, E.R. and L. Mollick. 2022. *New Modes of Learning Enabled by AI Chatbots: Three Methods and Assignments.* https://cetl.uconn.edu/wp-content/ uploads/sites/1775/2023/02/ChatGPT_AI_Chatbots.pdf.

Nadworny, R. n.d. "Facilitation Matrix for Better Workshops or Meetings." Medium. https://rnadworny.medium.com/facilitation-matrix-for-better-workshops-or-meetings-55da436f67ed.

Norman, D. and P.J. Stappers. March 2016. "DesignX: Complex Sociotechnical Systems." *She Ji: The Journal of Design, Economics, and Innovation* 1, no. 2, pp. 83106. https://doi.org/10.1016/j.sheji.2016.01.002.

"Obama to Graduates: Cultivate Empathy." 2006. Northwestern University. www.northwestern.edu/newscenter/stories/2006/06/barack.html.

Phan, T. 2023. "Nike, Tiffany and The 3% Rule." SatPost. www.readtrung .com/p/nike-tiffany-and-the-3-rule.

Picard, L. 2022. "Let's Have a (Disco) Ball." The New York Times. www.nytimes .com/2022/04/26/style/disco-ball-comeback.html.

Popova, M. 2013. "How Creativity in Humor, Art, and Science Works: Arthur Koestler's Theory of Bisociation." The Marginalian. www.themarginalian .org/2013/05/20/arthur-koestler-creativity-bisociation/.

Popper, K.R. 1966. "Of Clouds and Clocks: An Approach to the Problem of Rationality and the Freedom of Man."

Quarles, L. n.d. "The Key to Innovation: Challenging the Status Quo." Frog Design. www.frog.co/designmind/the-key-to-innovation-challenging-the-status-quo.

Radparvar, Jessica M. 2012. "Behind the Label: The Ideologies Behind The Lululemon Manifesto." HuffPost. www.huffpost.com/entry/behind-the-label-the-ideo_b_1922768.

Salazar, K. 2020. "7 Ways to Analyze a Customer-Journey Map." Nielsen Norman Group. www.nngroup.com/articles/analyze-customer-journey-map/.

Schoemaker, P.J. and P.E. Tetlock. 2016. *Superforecasting: How to Upgrade Your Company's Judgment.* Harvard Business Review. https://hbr.org/2016/05 /superforecasting-how-to-upgrade-your-companys-judgment.

Sharot, T. 2011. "The Optimism Bias." Time. https://content.time.com/time/health/article/0,8599,2074067,00.html.

Silbert, J. 2017. "Watch Virgil Abloh's Lecture at Harvard Graduate School of Design." Hypebeast. https://hypebeast.com/2017/10/virgil-abloh-harvard-lecture-video.

Sime, C. 2019. "Why Is It Hard To Start With The End In Mind?" Forbes. www.forbes.com/sites/carleysime/2019/01/29/why-is-it-hard-to-start-with-the-end-in-mind/?sh=7a55afa76cec.

Singletary, N. 2023. "How to Harness the Power of Love & Breakup Letters in UX Research." UX Planet. https://uxplanet.org/how-to-harness-the-power-of-love-breakup-letters-in-ux-research-ee0cb4cadde3.

Singleton, J. March 2015. "Head, Heart and Hands Model for Transformative Learning: Place as Context for Changing Sustainability Values." *The Journal of Sustainability Education.*

Sipos, Y., B. Battisti, B., and K. Grimm. 2008. "Achieving Transformative Sustainability Learning: Engaging Head, Hands and Heart." *International Journal of Sustainability in Higher Education* 9, no. 6886.

Skinner, S. 2022. "Mind the Gap: Gen Z Is Seeking 'Main-Character Energy' in 2023—Literally and Figuratively." McKinsey. www.mckinsey.com/~/media/mckinsey/email/genz/2022/12/20/2022-12-20aa.html.

Skrok, D. 2022. "Understand Color Symbolism | IxDF." The Interaction Design Foundation. www.interaction-design.org/literature/article/understand-color-symbolism.

Stafford, C.L. and J.F. Suri. 2021. "Insights for Innovation." IDEO U. www.ideou.com/products/insights-for-innovation?utm_feeditemid=&utm_device=c&utm_term=ideo%20insights%20for%20innovation&utm_source=google&utm_medium=cpc&utm_campaign=BOF+-+IDEO+Course+Themes+(PSDW)&hsa_cam=11993830240&hsa_grp=121226726532&hsa_mt=e&.

"Assume a Beginner's Mindset." n.d. Stanford d.school http://web.stanford.edu/~mshanks/MichaelShanks/files/508070.pdf.

"Cultivating Reflection and Metacognition." n.d. Sweetland Center for Writing, University of Michigan. https://lsa.umich.edu/content/dam/sweetland-assets/sweetland-documents/teachingresources/CultivatingReflectionand Metacognition/Metacognition.pdf.

Thompson, D. 2017. "The Four-Letter Code to Selling Just About Anything." The Atlantic. www.theatlantic.com/magazine/archive/2017/01/what-makes-things-cool/508772/.

Trudeau, L. 2022. "Develop a Go-to-Market Strategy Unit." Trailhead. https://trailhead.salesforce.com/content/learn/modules/go-to-market-planning/develop-a-go-to-market-strategy.

"What are Design Sprints?" 2020. Interaction Design Foundation. www
.interaction-design.org/literature/topics/design-sprints.

"When Are Consumers Most Likely to Feel Overwhelmed by Their Options?"
2017. Kellogg.

Insight. https://insight.kellogg.northwestern.edu/article/what-predicts-consumer-
choice-overload.

Victore, J. 2019. *Feck Perfuction: Dangerous Ideas on the Business of Life (Business
Books, Graphic Design Books, Books on Success)*. N.p.: Chronicle Books.

Whiting, K. and H. Park. 2023. "This Is Why "Polycrisis" Is a Useful Way of
Looking at the World Right Now." World Economic Forum. www.weforum
.org/agenda/2023/03/polycrisis-adam-tooze-historian-explains/.

Wong, E. 2022. "What Are Wicked Problems and How Might We Solve Them?"
The Interaction Design Foundation. www.interaction-design.org/literature
/article/wicked-problems-5-steps-to-help-you-tackle-wicked-problems-by-
combining-systems-thinking-with-agile-methodology.

Yeo, D. 2023. "Double Diamond v4.1: An Operating Manual for Designers
Using AI." UX Design. https://uxdesign.cc/double-diamond-version-4-1-an-
operating-manual-for-design-innovators-using-ai-c09cfa84b6be.

About the Author

Stacy is a Senior Lecturer and Director of Experiential Learning at Loyola University Chicago in the Quinlan School of Business. Her signature enthusiasm for co-designing projects with undergraduates and community client partners is well known and loved. She deeply believes design thinking practices embedded into experiential learning prepare students for today's workplace needs. Stacy was the first-ever teaching track faculty to receive both the Outstanding Instructor for Undergraduate Business Education and the Kolvenbach Award for Engaged Teaching. Nominated by her design thinking students, she was the inaugural winner of the Adolfo Nicolas SJ Excellence in Engaged Learning and Teaching Award. An active board member with Chicago Fair Trade and Rogers Park Business Alliance, Stacy is also a content strategist with PinPoint Collective, a women-owned, women-centered creative research and strategy studio. She lives in Chicago with her husband Matt and their French Bulldog Twombly.

Index

OTHER TITLES IN THE MARKETING COLLECTION

Naresh Malhotra, Georgia Tech, Editor

- *Proximity Marketing* by Rajagopal
- *Winning With Strategic Marketing* by David Altounian and Mike Cronin
- *Brand Positioning With Power* by Robert S. Gordon
- *Multicultural Marketing Is Your Story* by Eliane Karsaklian
- *Marketing of Consumer Financial Products* by Ritu Srivastava
- *The Big Miss* by Zhecho Dobrev
- *Digital Brand Romance* by Anna Harrison
- *Brand Vision* by James Everhart
- *Brand Naming* by Rob Meyerson
- *Fast Fulfillment* by Sanchoy Das
- *Multiply Your Business Value Through Brand & AI* by Rajan Narayan
- *Branding & AI* by Chahat Aggarwal
- *The Business Design Cube* by Rajagopal
- *Customer Relationship Management* by Michael Pearce

Concise and Applied Business Books

The Collection listed above is one of 30 business subject collections that Business Expert Press has grown to make BEP a premiere publisher of print and digital books. Our concise and applied books are for...

- Professionals and Practitioners
- Faculty who adopt our books for courses
- Librarians who know that BEP's Digital Libraries are a unique way to offer students ebooks to download, not restricted with any digital rights management
- Executive Training Course Leaders
- Business Seminar Organizers

Business Expert Press books are for anyone who needs to dig deeper on business ideas, goals, and solutions to everyday problems. Whether one print book, one ebook, or buying a digital library of 110 ebooks, we remain the affordable and smart way to be business smart. For more information, please visit www.businessexpertpress.com, or contact sales@businessexpertpress.com.